Milton and the Muses

MILTON
and the Muses

E. R. GREGORY

THE UNIVERSITY
OF ALABAMA PRESS
TUSCALOOSA AND LONDON

Copyright © 1989 by
The University of Alabama Press
Tuscaloosa, Alabama 35487

ALL RIGHTS RESERVED

Manufactured in the United States of America
Designed by Laury A. Egan

Library of Congress Cataloging-in-Publication Data

Gregory, E. R.
Milton and the muses.
Bibliography: p.   Includes index.
1. Milton, John, 1608–1674—Knowledge—Folklore, mythology. 2. Muses (Greek deities) in literature.
I. Title.
PR3592.M73G7   1989   821'.4   86-30842
ISBN 0-8173-0362-6

*British Library Cataloguing-in-Publication
Data is available.*

This study is dedicated in affection and admiration
to three gentlemen-scholars:
Waldo F. McNeir
Jackson I. Cope
and Aubrey L. Williams.
In a profession—and indeed a world—that offers
little help in the defining of values,
they helped me to define my own.

CONTENTS

	PREFACE	ix
1.	Tradition and the Individual Talent	1
2.	The Tender Stops of Various Quills	13
3.	The Mellowing Year	44
4.	Long Choosing and Beginning Late	73
5.	Heav'nly Muse	94
6.	In His Blindness Seeing All	125
	NOTES	134
	BIBLIOGRAPHY	156
	INDEX	168

PREFACE

THIS STUDY has been many years in the making. Retrospectively, I see its origins in a doctoral dissertation, "Du Bartas and the Modes of Christian Poetry in England," written at the University of Oregon in the early sixties; and portions of the present work were completed as long ago as 1974 when I read a small piece of it at the Wisconsin Milton Tercentenaries. Inevitably, however, years of reading John Milton, teaching him, and mulling over problems supposedly solved in long completed work have wrought a considerable change in emphasis from the more narrowly philological concerns of my doctoral study. The present work focuses far less on establishing what Milton read—most of that was done long ago anyway—and far more on how he read—a matter about which even yet there is far less certainty.

In this, as in other ways, it participates in the critical trends of the last decade. A small library of books has appeared in recent years, each of them probing Milton's relation to tradition or to earlier writers such as Spenser, Ovid, Shakespeare, even though the data for assessing these relationships was all gathered many years ago. In the background of these studies stand such giants of contemporary criticism as Harold Bloom and Stanley Fish. No critic today can consider such matters as how an author reads earlier writers or how a community of interpreters affects that author's work or our understanding of it without taking into account the work of these men. Closer yet, the admirable studies of William Kerrigan in some ways cover the same territory as my own.

My own presuppositions and approaches, however, are vastly different from these gentlemen, so that I have preferred on the whole to do my own work in my own way. In bringing earlier criticism into my discussion, my principle has been to select what maximally would illuminate the thin line where past and present meet in authorial creation. Milton's use of

Preface

tradition, his sense of audience, his developing awareness of the inspirational process, the maturing of his art—these are matters of such importance to our own age as to justify great effort in order perhaps to understand them only marginally better. For all the years involved in writing it, this study should be considered more as an essay designed to illustrate how Milton used the materials he inherited rather than as an exhaustive study of Muse lore in his writings. Thus, I have not treated nor even listed all his references to the Muses, and I eliminated from the final draft revised versions of earlier published work on the ground that their content did not add to that illumination sought.

IT IS a pleasure now to thank each of the many individuals who assisted me over the years spent in researching and writing this book. My greatest debt, of course, is to those professors to whom the book is dedicated, Waldo F. McNeir, who directed my doctoral work at Oregon, and Jackson Cope and Aubrey Williams with whom I studied at Rice University. For long continuing support in the form of grants and sabbaticals, I must thank the University of Toledo. Such enlightened administrators as Harold L. Allen, Alfred A. Cave, Robert J. Niedzielski, and David G. Hoch have been generous both in financial support and in encouragement at a time when funding for research in the humanities has never been more difficult to come by. In its final stages, Professors Michael Manheim and Harriet F. Adams read and criticized individual chapters to great improvement. Robin Smith provided invaluable assistance in checking quotations and preparing the index. Finally, my wife, Martha, brought to its proofreading the expertise that can only come from years spent as a professional cataloger.

Portions of this study appeared earlier in *Milton Quarterly, Milton Studies,* and *Explorations in Renaissance Culture,* and are included with the permission of those journals' editors. The illustrations appear through the courtesy of their owners—the Trustees of the British Museum, the Lewis Collection of the Texas Christian University Library, the Department of Rare Books and Special Collections of the University of Michi-

Preface

gan Library, and a private collection. In the case of Figures 1 and 2, which appeared earlier in Raimond van Marle's *Iconographie de l'art profane au moyen age et à la renaissance*, vol. II, *Allégories et symboles* (The Hague, 1932), permission was also granted by that work's publisher, Martinus Nijhoff. Permission to quote from Allen Ginsberg's *Collected Poems* (New York, 1984) was given by Harper and Row and by Penguin Books International. Throughout the present study, the edition of Milton's poetry and prose cited is *The Works of John Milton*, ed. Frank Allen Patterson et al. (New York: Columbia University Press, 1931–38), referred to in the text as CM, and used with permission. No attempt has been made to reproduce the peculiarities of Renaissance printing.

Milton and the Muses

Tradition and the Individual Talent

THE FOLLOWING STUDY is a book-length elaboration of as vintage a commonplace as criticism has to offer—that John Milton is at one and the same time the most traditional and the most individual of poets. William Hazlitt said it long ago: "Milton has borrowed more than any other writer, and exhausted every source of imitation, sacred or profane; yet he is perfectly distinct from every other writer. He is a writer of centos, and yet in originality scarcely inferior to Homer."[1] Rosemond Tuve said it thirty years ago: "He is in the highest degree an original poet, and nothing we can call by a name in him but can be named in another; he differs from everyone, and in everything does what others had done. The final accomplishments are more mature and profound than experiment and innovation could produce, and oddly enough they awaken more astonishment."[2] And only three years ago the editors of *Milton Studies* said it yet once more, rephrasing the thought, interestingly enough, in language much older than Milton himself: "It was while Milton was still working in the medium of Latin . . . that . . . he mastered the art of transforming flowers culled from various sources into honey that was all his own."[3] Indeed, considering how many others have said it and the variety of ways it has been said, the reader may well question the need for yet another exposition of a point that everyone more or less agrees on.

The answer to that lies in the nature of commonplace itself: unless constantly rethought, it loses its ability to illuminate;

Milton and the Muses

and its perception, originally won through careful reading and painful thinking, reifies through repetition into thoughtless and uncritical admiration. If this peculiar gift of Milton's is worth understanding, if like most gifts, it was perfected through practice, we should do more than pay homage to Hazlitt or Tuve before passing on to current studies that relate him to Marxist struggle, contemporary poetry, modern philosophy.[4] We should clothe their generalization in fresh particulars or discard it altogether.

As long as any interest inheres in defining more sharply the distinction between what Milton inherited and what he created, no more fitting area of investigation exists than Milton's use of the Muses. The lore surrounding the nine daughters of Zeus and Memory was ancient and extensive; his revision of it, an impressive transformation of unoriginal material into original art. The area, in short, offers precisely that vast array of particulars needed to make this old perception our own. It constitutes the subject matter of this book.

THE MUSES enter Western literature very close to its beginnings, making their first appearance in Hesiod's *Theogony*, written probably in the late seventh century B.C. Hesiod relates how they came upon him as he was pasturing his flock in the foothills of Mount Helikon and inspired him, "base shepherd" that he was, to write great poetry. Their function, their parentage, their individual names even, all these are in the opening lines of the *Theogony*, nor has anyone ever done better in conveying the poet's sense that his work originates outside himself and is not his to claim.[5]

Whether the Muses in Hesiod were cunningly contrived personifications or "seen and heard in hallucination," as our contemporary Julian Jaynes has argued, is a matter of debate.[6] What is not debatable is that the Muses incarnated the suprarational dimension of the intellectual life so satisfyingly that they survived long after any literal belief in them was possible, survived even the hostility that early Christian writers directed toward them and pagan mythology in general. Protean-like, they adapted themselves to a variety of meanings.

2

Tradition and the Individual Talent

For Plato, they originated the divine fury that alone could guarantee poetic excellence:

> There is a . . . form of possession or madness, of which the Muses are the source. This seizes a tender, virgin soul and stimulates it to rapt passionate expression, especially in lyric poetry, glorifying the countless mighty deeds of ancient times for the instruction of posterity. But if any man come to the gates of poetry without the madness of the Muses, persuaded that skill alone will make him a good poet, then shall he and his works of sanity with him be brought to nought by the poetry of madness, and behold, their place is nowhere to be found.[7]

For Cicero, on the other hand, they were associated with the quietly satisfying life of the thinker. In comparing Archimedes with the Syracusan tyrant, Dionysius, he asked rhetorically:

> Who in the world, who enjoys merely some degree of communion with the Muses, that is to say with liberal education and refinement, is there who would not choose to be this mathematician rather than that tyrant?[8]

At the very end of the classical world, some writers like Paulinus of Nola (353/4–431 A.D.) rejected them in their poetry because they were part of a false religion, but on the whole the more sensible position of Augustine, that truth is truth whatever its provenance, prevailed:

> We should not think that we ought not to learn literature because Mercury is said to be its inventor, nor that because the pagans dedicated temples to Justice and Virtue and adored in stones what should be performed in the heart, we should therefore avoid justice and virtue. Rather, every good and true Christian should understand that wherever he may find truth, it is his Lord's.[9]

Thus the Muses, though occasionally subjected to hostile scrutiny, survived. The classical literature wherein they appeared contained, quite simply, too generous a portion of the world's truth to die.

Indeed, classical literature not only survived, but remained in Milton's day—as it had been for two thousand years—the staple of education in Western Europe. *Musa, –ae* was one of the first Latin words he learned, for it was the paradigm of first-declension nouns in William Lily's "official" Latin grammar; and from the time he learned it at age six or seven to the end of his life, the Muses were never far from his consciousness. In his scholarly work, he never lost an interest in the kind of material he had learned about them in grammar school and indeed labored sporadically for some years on a "New Thesaurus Linguae Latinae, according to the manner of Stephanus"; a work that by the middle 1650s, "he had been long since Collecting from his own Reading, and still went on with it at times, even very near to his dying day."[10]

In his own writing, the Muses appear early, often, and late, but his references to them change markedly over the years. The ones in his early Latin poetry, for example, are conventional. They reveal that the Muses, like much else in classical mythology, were initially for Milton a kind of poetic shorthand, a way of saying certain things quickly and formulaically so that they were immediately understood by the audience for whom they were intended. Working even within the narrow confines of Latin composition, however, he early learned how to put his own individuating touch on the absolutely unoriginal phrases, epithets, and figures that he used. Not surprisingly, he is longer in learning how to take over large myths and rework them in terms of his poetic needs; but this too comes with the passage of time. Its most striking manifestations, of course, are the prologues to *Paradise Lost,* where he adapts the myths of the blind bard and his Muse to his own circumstances with surprising results. The materials out of which he builds these passages are as traditional as one could wish, but their effect is not to make the reader think of Du Bartas, Spenser, Tasso, Prudentius, or anyone else. Rather, they rivet his attention on John Milton's act of seeking and receiving the inspiration that alone can enable him to finish his work. One might say that he heightens the significance of his personal situation through the traditional materials in which he clothes it, but the relation is reciprocal. The traditional materials are vivified by his incorporating them into his own experience. In any event, the effect is quite different from any other writer's utilization of the same materials.

As with all areas of Miltonic scholarship, Milton's use of Muse lore is not exactly *terra incognita*. Portions of it indeed have been traversed rather often. The identity of Milton's Muse in *Paradise Lost*, for example, has occasioned much commentary.[11] None of the studies yet done, however, integrates Milton's writing about her with his education, his life, or his sense of audience. The results have been at best a partial illumination of her nature; at worst, a sad misdirection of energy and ability. When a scholar like Harry F. Robins concludes, on his knowledge of Origen, that Milton's Urania is really Jesus Christ, one can only object that he has turned Milton from a learned writer, which he undoubtedly was, into an arcane one, which he was not. True enough, Milton says it is "the meaning, not the Name" of Urania that he invokes; but that meaning must root itself in materials he and a substantial portion of his audience intimately share, or he fails in his purpose of writing in a public genre like epic. The fitness of the fit audience though few for whom Milton wrote depended on its aptness to receive moral instruction and not in specialized knowledge of the Church Fathers.

The present study essays, then, to integrate background and foreground more thoroughly than its predecessors. If it does only that, it has justified itself for the small circle of Milton scholars most apt to read it. In my view, however, it has significance for all those who ponder the fate of poetry in our own time. It begins by examining an educational system that by our standards was incredibly rigid, prescriptive, dull, and irrelevant and ends by suggesting that comprehension of that system helps in understanding our own cultural predicament. The help offered is, of course, limited. The role of literary history is not to ring the bell backward nor suggest that the restoration of old educational policies would necessarily solve our problems. The most it can do is suggest some ways in which perhaps we are wrong, some ways in which maybe the culture of Milton's day was more conducive to the writing of poetry than our own is. A respected colleague of mine, for example, speaks for many when he suggests that terms like metaphor, simile, metonymy, personification, synecdoche, tropes, appositive, hyperbole, and the like, are of little use in helping students to write poetry:

> They can be useful for advanced critics and theorists, but they are most commonly used as instruments for the torture of children. They make it possible for teachers who know nothing about literature to fill their time, to bore their charges, and to grade examinations in the safest and least time-consuming manner. A metaphor is a comparison. That is all you know—and all you need to know.[12]

One shudders to think what his response would be to a system that routinely taught seven- and eight-year olds all of the above and a host of other terms from anaphora to zeugma as well.

But surely, some readers will object, that is not what made Milton great. Of course not, but the underlying premise behind this plethora of terminology—that the more rigorously the techniques of good writing were analyzed the likelier the prospect of teaching them successfully—was by no means absurd. Coupled with unremitting drill, it enabled persons of moderate talent to achieve a level of competence in prose and verse alike that most of us today can only envy. Its effect on a talented and strong-minded writer like Milton is more problematic but still considerable.

To be sure, Milton himself does not seem to have thought much of his education. He easily enough grasped its weakness, that it too easily deteriorated into the kind of mindless pedantry my colleague rightly deplores. Being, like all of us, a prisoner of time, he did not accurately gauge its strengths. Thus he accused his political opponent, Salmasius, of substituting the shadowy paraphernalia of scholarship for its substance:

> A learned man?—you that even unto your old age seem rather to have turned over phrase-books and lexicons and glossaries than to have perused good authors with judgment or profit; . . .

while overlooking the fact that he himself had made abundant use of such materials.[13] Had he been asked to defend himself on this point, he would probably have replied that he had used them as aids in understanding and remembering his reading, not as tools to gull his audience into thinking he had read more than in point of fact he had. Of future systems when phrase-books, lexicons, and glossaries would be items as exotic to grammar-school children as ferules and duncecaps, he was quite unprescient. The ideal system he sketched in his tractate *Of Education,* for all its differences, is much closer to the system in which he was educated than to ours.

Admittedly, material such as grammar-school exercises sheds only partial light on the view of Milton and his poetry that this study affirms: that he is an intensely personal poet whose personality and art cannot be studied as separate entities. Such a view needs qualification, of course. Milton's work is not so embarrassingly intimate as some of today's writers, and precedent exists for such personal elements as it does include; but the thrust of the present study, like many others, is to render such precedent inadequate. Re the prologues themselves, they are admittedly not a verbatim transcript of Milton's creative processes. Although he makes it sound, for example, as if he were merely the Muse's amanuensis, I do not argue that no planning or revision went into his poetry, only that the effect of careful craftsmanship in the three great poems owes more to a lifetime of disciplined work than to excruciating pains lavished on them at the time of composition.

Elsewhere in his writings, "he reverenced workmanship, and insisted upon method"; so that Ida Langdon, trying to systematize *Milton's Theory of Poetry and Fine Art,* concluded that "we may consider his tributes to inspiration, spontaneity, and inborn aptitude to be the concessive or modifying elements in his theory."[14] This may have been true prior to his writing of *Paradise Lost.* It was not true at its conclusion for reasons that the prologues read in conjunction with an account of his life make clear. Here as elsewhere, then, our response to the poetry cannot be separated from our response to the man. The prologues are a heightened and ordered version of the truth as Milton perceived it and should not be read in isolation from our knowledge and response to their author.

Milton himself desired no such isolation. Often cited as proof of this is his statement "that he who would not be frustrate of his hope to write well hereafter in laudable things, ought him selfe to bee a true Poem."[15] More to the point is a later passage indicating success in that regard:

> Many have made a figure by their published writings whose living voice and daily conversation have presented next to nothing that was not low and common: if, then, I can attain the distinction of seeming myself equal in mind and manners to any writings of mine that have been tolerably to the purpose, there will be the double effect that I shall so have added weight personally to my writings, and shall receive back by way of reflection from them credit, how small soever it may be, yet greater in proportion. For, in that case, whatever is right and laudable in them, that same I shall seem not more to have derived from authors of high excellence than to have fetched forth pure and sincere from the inmost feelings of my own mind and soul.[16]

At present, there is a greater awareness of the impossibility of such an isolation than there has been in decades. Twenty years ago, for example, it seemed a bit quaint of William Riley Parker to begin his biography with the observation

> that any attempt to distinguish between Milton the Poet and Milton the Man is foredoomed to failure. The invisible line sometimes supposed to exist between literary criticism and enlightened biography of a literary figure defies detection in this instance. Milton's developing personality demands recognition in most of his early verse, and in his more mature compositions the artist and the man are inseparable.[17]

Today, however, this perception bids fair to be the orthodoxy of the moment, to the extent that any one position can be considered orthodox in an era and profession so fragmented as our own.

Tradition and the Individual Talent

Forty years ago, James Holly Hanford, taking into account the attitudes of the great Modernists, could proclaim as self-evident truth "that Milton, despite the wish so often voiced that he might be living at this hour, is truly of the past."[18] Even as Hanford wrote, however, new poets were appearing, caring little for "objectivity" and more sympathetic by far toward Milton's personality and art than were Pound or Eliot. Among them, none has complimented Milton more handsomely than Allen Ginsberg, who considers him preeminent in a pantheon of personal writers who speak powerfully to writers like himself:

> Here I am naked without identity
> with no more body than the fine black tracery of pen
> mark on soft paper
> as star talks to star multiple beams of sunlight all
> the same myriad thought
> in one fold of the universe where Whitman was
> and Blake and Shelley saw Milton dwelling as in a
> starry temple
> brooding in his blindness seeing all.[19]

Poets like Ginsberg and critics like the late Joan Webber, who early recognized what was happening, thus led the way toward a new appreciation of the old truth embodied in Parker's comment. Certainly the last ten years have seen handsomely documented studies that trace connections between Milton's life and work in startlingly various ways. Works that have little else in common such as Mary Ann Radzinowicz's *Toward "Samson Agonistes"* and William Kerrigan's *The Sacred Complex* yet unite in a common understanding that study of Milton's life and work must go forward together.[20] In keeping with this heightened awareness of Milton's selfhood, studies of his reading in recent years have gone far beyond merely establishing that he read this or that author and that this line or that feature reveals the earlier author's influence. Joseph Anthony Wittreich, Jr.'s *Visionary Poetics*, John Guillory's *Poetic Authority*, Maureen Quilligan's *Milton's Spenser*, Richard J. DuRocher's *Milton and Ovid*, Paul Stevens's *Imagination and the Presence of Shakespeare in Paradise Lost*—such studies have sought rather to enlarge our understanding of the reading process itself in so intensely individual an author, how he understood, assimilated, and altered his predecessors to express what he himself had to say.[21]

And now this study, which reflects a like concern. To say that the man and his work are inseparable is to imply a strong, unifying personality that put its stamp on all it touched from his juvenilia to *Paradise Lost*. Even the strongest of personalities, however, are themselves shaped by the cultural milieu in which they find themselves. Milton's culture, particularly in the agency of its schools, accounts for the traditional nature of his work. In those schools, neither composition nor reading was taught so as to encourage individuality of response or expression. To say this is to overstate the matter just a bit. As always, the talent of the teacher was more important than the educational doctrine dominant at the moment. To most schoolboys, for instance, the widely practiced exercise of imitation involved nothing more than the stultifying and mechanical reproduction of images and phrases from the great masters. In the hands of a sensitive teacher, however, imitation could become a free—one might say individual—rendering of those masters' form and spirit.[22] Perhaps Milton's tribute to Thomas Young pointed toward some such achievement on Young's part.

> He led the way for me, when first I traversed Aonia's retreats and the holy greensward of the twice-cleft ridge, [he led the way for me] when I drank Pieria's waters, and, favored by Clio, I thrice sprinkled my happy lips with Castalia's wine.[23]

The tribute is a touching one, and its meaning and the classical terms in which it is couched will be examined in some detail in Chapter 5. In all likelihood, however, Young's role, while important, was at most that of facilitator, a person who helped Milton in finding a little sooner his own unique voice.

If, then, Milton's education shaped him, more important by far is the fact that he shaped his education to his own ends and needs. To clarify the way he did this, let us return for a moment to Hazlitt, where the passage with which we began continues in the following vein:

> The quantity of art in him shews the strength of his genius: the weight of his intellectual obligations would have oppressed any other writer. Milton's learning has the effect of intuition. He describes objects, of which he could only have read in books, with the vividness of actual observation. (*Complete Works*, 5: 58–59)

To phrase the matter differently, one might say that Milton read as he wrote—as his own person. For his peers, writers like Cicero, Ovid, Virgil were so great and remote as to be literally inimitable regardless of the number of technical exercises in imitation that they completed. Milton, on the other hand, had no such hobbling sense of inferiority. To say even that these writers were his friends is to imply a greater distance than in fact existed. He simply incorporated them into himself and thought no more about "using" them. Consequently, when he did use them, it was always in new, surprising, and individual ways.

As his masters had used the Muses, so did he, up to a point. Any poet in Milton's day could claim a Muse, and most did; but their long reign was ending. A few die-hard Puritans like William Dell insisted that they and all pagan gods and goddesses were the work of the devil and that it was

> most necessary . . . that Christians should forget the names of their gods and muses, which were but devils and damned creatures, and all their mythology and fabulous inventions and let them all go to Satan from whence they came.[24]

A more potent threat by far, however, came from those thinkers like Thomas Hobbes who were beginning to subject the Muses to the kind of rational scrutiny that in the next century would finish them off even as poetic clichés. Such thinkers scorned them not for any melodramatic reason like their being the work of the devil, but rather on the ground that, coolly considered, they were intellectually discredited and literarily demodé. Building on the old perception that such figures were pagan personifications of natural phenomena, Hobbes was quite tolerant of their usage in older writers but saw no necessity for it in those sharing his own incomparable modernity. Thus in his "Answer to the Preface to Gondibert," he defended Davenant for dispensing with the practice:

> In that you make so small account of the example of almost all the approved poets, ancient and modern, who thought fit in the beginning, and sometimes also in the progress of their poems, to invoke a Muse, or some other deity, that should dictate to them, or assist them in their writings; they that take not the laws of art, from any reason of their own, but from the fashion of precedent times, will perhaps accuse your singularity. For my part, I neither subscribe to their accusation, nor yet condemn that heathen custom, otherwise than as accessory to their false religion. For their poets were their divines; had the name of prophets; exercised amongst the people a kind of spiritual authority; would be thought to speak by a divine spirit; have their works which they writ in verse . . . pass for the word of God, and not of man, and to be hearkened to with reverence. . . . But why a Christian should think it an ornament to his poem, either to profane the true God, or invoke a false one, I can imagine no cause, but a reasonless imitation of custom . . . by which a man enabled to speak wisely from the principles of nature, and his own meditation, loves rather to be thought to speak by inspiration, like a bagpipe.[25]

Thus, we now know, indifference was to achieve what hatred could not. For the time being, however, most poets continued to invoke a Muse, although their invocations, being merely formulaic, were stale and uninteresting. How different were the results that Milton achieved in *Paradise Lost*. By concentrating on "the meaning, not the Name," by adapting the materials he had inherited to his own particular circumstances, he endowed his own Muse, Urania, with fresh life and made her once again—and for the last time in Western literature—a creature of power and mystery.

The Tender Stops of Various Quills

FAMILY, teachers, culture all encouraged Milton in his seriousness, industry, systematic cast of mind, and above all in his gift for language. Other elements necessary for the creation of his own great work they did not much encourage—the idiosyncratic nature of his genius and a healthy awareness of the suprarational's role in creating his art, for example. He was therefore a lifetime in coming to terms with the more personal and less structured dimension of his art that finds full expression in the major works. In the beginning, however, he learned about the Muses in an atmosphere that seemingly mocked all the values those lovely ladies were thought to stand for. What he learned about them, how he learned it, and how that learning worked its way into the more derivative portions of his writing, these are the main concerns of this chapter; and whatever illuminates them—details, speculation even, about character, family, teachers, culture—is included.

SERIOUS TO LEARN AND KNOW

Some have taken Jesus' meditative words in *Paradise Regain'd* as applicable to Milton himself:

> When I was yet a child, no childish play
> To me was pleasing, all my mind was set
> Serious to learn and know, and thence to do
> What might be publick good.[1]

This is unlikely. The boy Milton probably did find some childish play pleasing just as in later years the blind bard manifested a charm and humor in social intercourse that posterity too easily forgot. Still, he seems by nature to have been an essentially serious youth. His nephew, Edward Phillips, tells us that he succeeded in school "not more by the Discipline of the School and good Instructions of his Masters . . . than by his own happy Genius, prompt Wit and Apprehension, and insuperable Industry" (*Early Lives*, pp. 53–54).

All this is probably true enough. He lived, after all, in an age that did not prize gaiety or spontaneity in children as subsequent ages have; and although his parents loved him and praised his efforts lavishly, they were of a time and class that heartily endorsed the Biblical observation: "Foolishness *is* bound in the heart of a child; *but* the rod of correction shall drive it far from him" (Prov. 22:15). Their time and class moreover dictated that hard work was not only a practical necessity but a religious duty so that the parable of the talents, so meaningful to Milton as an adult, undoubtedly worked its way deep into his consciousness while he was still a child.

Beyond that, his parents were getting on in years and had lost at least one earlier child before he was born, facts that undoubtedly contributed to the pride they took in their healthy and intelligent son.[2] More difficult to assess, but probably more important, were the character and circumstances of Milton's father. A man of artistic abilities who had had to earn his own way in the world and supported himself and his family in a remunerative but pedestrian profession, he hoped perhaps that his son could have the intellectual life that he himself would have preferred.[3] Be that as it may, the Miltons destined their son for the ministry and provided him an education far in excess of what he needed to excel even in that most learned of professions.[4]

As for his education, however severe its limitations, it certainly fostered both industry and a highly organized approach to learning. Not surprisingly, then, by the time he was twelve years old, Milton was staying up every night till twelve, expending his energies "as well in voluntary Improvements of his own choice, as the exact perfecting of his School-Exercises"; and the cast of mind these comments imply remained with him ever after (*Early Lives*, p. 54).

The earliest comments on his character that have survived attest to this cast of mind. They appear in letters to him from his friend, Charles Diodati. Although the function of these letters, which are in Greek, was partly to display their author's erudition, they also expressed feelings and perceptions that, doubtless, were sincere. From them we learn that Milton in his late teens impressed his best friend as a serious and studious young man:

> Why do you despise the gifts of nature? Why inexcusably persist in hanging over books and studies all day and all night? Live, laugh make the most of youth and the hours; and cease studying the zeals and recreations and indolences of the wise men of old, wearing yourself out the while. I, in all things else inferior to you, in this one thing, in knowing when to set a measure to my labors, both seem to myself, and am, your better.[5]

As to Milton's approach to his studies, his own letters to Diodati, written some years later, afford interesting insights; for they reveal that he conceived these studies systematically and pursued them rigorously. Excusing himself for his tardiness in writing, Milton compared his approach to study with his friend's:

> I know your method of studying to be so arranged that you frequently take breath in the middle, visit your friends, write much, sometimes make a journey whereas my genius is such that no delay, no rest, no care or thought almost of anything, holds me aside until I reach the end I am making for, and round off, as it were, some great period of my studies.[6]

Again in his next letter:

> I have by continuous reading brought down the affairs of the Greeks as far as to the time when they ceased to be Greeks. I have been long engaged in the obscure business of the state of Italians under the Longobards, the Franks,

and the Germans, down to the time when liberty was granted them by Rodolph, King of Germany: from that period it will be better to read separately what each City did by its own wars.[7]

Such was the character of the youth—grave, industrious, systematic in his approach to learning.

His forte obviously lay in the arts of language, and in this he was singularly fortunate with regard to the system in which he was schooled. Early on, he demonstrated a remarkable talent for composition, particularly versification. The most precise dating of this development occurs in John Aubrey's notes, where it is related to the portrait painted of him when he was ten: "1619, he was ten yeares old, as by his picture: & was then a Poet" (*Early Lives,* p. 2). If this is true, it indicates some precocity; for although the chronology of his grammar-school education is not clear, he was probably in his third year of schooling at that time, and poetry-writing—or, more accurately, versification—was not begun until the fifth year.[8]

Milton's own words on the matter in *Reason of Church-Government* are less precise as to date but more to the point in stressing the quality of these early productions:

> I must say therefore that after I had from my first yeeres by the ceaselesse diligence and care of my father, whom God recompence, bin exercis'd to the tongues, and some sciences, as my age would suffer, by sundry masters and teachers both at home and at the schools, it was found that whether ought was impos'd me by them that had the overlooking, or betak'n to of mine own choise in English, or other tongue, prosing or versing, but chiefly this latter, the stile by certain vital signes it had, was likely to live. (CM, 3: 235)

Some corroboration of the excellence of these early productions may be had from Milton's brother, Christopher, although his recollections may have been colored by Milton's own words and his subsequent fame as a poet:

> When he went to Schoole, when he was very young he studied very hard and sate-up very late, comonly till 12 or

one aclock at night . . . and in those yeares composed many Copies of verses, which might well become a riper age.[9]

The Usual Method of Teaching Arts

Now none of the characteristics documented above is surprising. Indeed, the most rigorous of scholars might well grant, solely on the basis of his mature work, that Milton as a child had a flair for language. Collectively, however, they illuminate how he not only fitted into an educational system that by today's standards was incredibly stultifying, but indeed turned the training he received there to good account as ultimately he found his own unique artistic voice. One might, in fact, argue that Milton was singularly fortunate with regard to the system in which he was schooled; for it was admirably equipped to help students like him whose talents were principally verbal and who were not afraid of hard work. Focused largely upon linguistic matters, it was geared toward helping such students achieve their full potential; and when it worked, as it did in Milton's case, it worked superbly.

The system's goal, as stated by Renaissance educators, was a moral one. For Erasmus, the end of learning was to teach the truth;[10] for Milton, it was "to repair the ruines of our first Parents by regaining to know God aright."[11] The connection between such ends and the daily grind of grammar-school life lay in the universally held conviction that the literature of Greece and Rome was more useful in teaching the truth and repairing the ruins of original sin than any other the world had produced. Because we can only learn truth through language, Erasmus argued, we do well to begin education with its study, specifically Greek and Latin, "since within these two literatures are contained all the knowledge which we recognize as of vital importance to mankind." Or in Milton's words: "seeing every Nation affords not experience and tradition enough for all kind of Learning, therefore we are chiefly taught the Languages of those people who have at any time been most industrious after Wisdom."

In practice, however, the emphasis often fell on mastery of the languages themselves rather than the wisdom they contained. Their mastery, particularly Latin, had practical ramifications that neither the schoolmaster nor the schoolboy could ignore.[12] Even in the seventeenth century, the ability effectively to use Latin in both its written and spoken forms was virtually a necessity for advancement in the learned professions, and to some extent, in society as a whole. Beyond that, most schoolmasters, had they been asked to justify their teaching on moral rather than practical grounds, would have argued that their students could grasp the truths contained in Latin and Greek literature only if they had completely mastered the languages themselves. Such justifications, however, were not often required. Consequently, while a few like Milton gave much thought to the relation between professed goals and pedagogical practice, the majority probably felt without giving the matter much thought that the centuries of precedent for their daily routine constituted sufficient rationale for continuing it. The end result was that even in a good school such as St. Paul's the emphasis fell heavily on linguistic command and little on the truths that these literatures might contain. The emphasis on memorization, the working over of the same materials ad nauseam, the gigantic paraphernalia of scholarly tools, the tremendous number of Latin compositions, prose and poetry alike, that the schoolboy was forced to write—all these make sense only when we realize that he studied, say, Cicero not as an eclectic Latin adapter of Greek philosophy nor yet as an interesting public figure in a troubled time, but in order to speak and write like Cicero.

Such were the goals, moral and practical, toward which his grammar-school activities were directed.[13] The standard age for him to begin those activities was seven. Prior to that, he had learned, either at home or in a petty school, how to read and write English. At age seven, he embarked on an eight-year course of study whose sole purpose was the teaching of the classical languages. History, geography, English literature, and much else were taught incidentally; but only Latin and Greek, and a little Hebrew in a few advanced schools like St. Paul's, were formally taught. The lines along which they were taught were those of the ancient and honorable trivium, grammar, rhetoric, and logic.

The schoolboy thus began his grammar-school days by memorizing William Lily's Latin grammar, whose usage in the school was mandated by law. Far more comprehensive than today's grammars, Lily included materials on figures of speech and prosody. After mastering the basics of grammar, the Accidents, the students learned the remainder of Lily in conjunction with easy reading assignments like Lily's own "Carmen de Moribus," the *Sententiae Pueriles,* and Cato's *Disticha Moralia.* The "Carmen" was an eighty-five line poem consisting of moral precepts; the *Sententiae* and Cato, collections of moralized sayings, beginning with two words and ranging up to full-length sentences. All had to be learned backwards and forwards. If given the Latin, the student had to translate it, give a full grammatical description of each word, and be prepared to decline or conjugate each word if asked.

From such sentences, he began at an early age the all-important "making of Latine," that is, learning to write Latin himself. He did this by taking English translations of these sentences and turning them back into Latin. The ideal was that he should reproduce on his own the words of the Latin original. Much effort was expended in helping him to achieve that goal so that very early he had to direct his attention toward connotation, levels of diction, historical appropriateness, tone. From such beginnings, in time and with luck, the student's own elaborate compositions flourished. In later stages of his education, he was exposed, if he attended a good school, to more sophisticated analysis of his texts including rhetorical considerations, prosodical analysis, and literary criticism; and his study broadened to include Greek in his fourth year and, possibly, Hebrew in his eighth. Always, however, he was held to the practice of memorizing his texts and of using them as the basis for his own compositions, at first prose and, later, poetry, written and then spoken.

Such, in outline, was the system. It offers ample targets for criticism; but our criticism should be to the point in terms of what the system was trying to do and not misdirected toward matter that, historically, is irrelevant. Irrelevant, for example, are picturesque descriptions of seven-year-old boys forced to sit eight hours a day, six days a week, summer and winter, on benches with no backs to them as they memorized text after text, urged on by the schoolmaster with his ever-present birch rod. Shakespeare summed up that dimension of the educational system in Jaques' thumbnail sketch of "the whining school-boy, with his satchel / And shining morning face, creeping like snail / Unwillingly to school." No one could blame the poor child, of course, knowing what awaited him, but such details merely reflect daily life in an era that, unlike our own, placed little value on creature comforts.

More substantive objections can be made to the system in terms of its failure to achieve its own end, the teaching of the classical languages. Taken on its own terms, it often failed. One of Milton's contemporaries, Adam Martindale, was lightly ironical as he described the results in his own case:

> Mine exercises were usually a piece of Latine . . . every day of the weeke, save Thursdays and Saturdays; and besides somewhat weekly as I rose in ability, first a dialogue in imitation of Corderius, or Pueriles Confabulatiunculae, then an epistle wherin I was to follow Cicero, though (alas!) at a great distance.[14]

Indeed, at its worst, the system actually led to students forgetting how to read English, an accomplishment that the petty school was supposed to teach them in one year prior to their coming to grammar school itself. Large portions of Lily's grammar were in Latin, and children were forced to memorize them without understanding what they were memorizing. Thus, Charles Hoole, one of the ablest teachers of the day, wrote:

> *The commonly received way to teach children the first rudiments of Latine-Speech is, to put them to read the Accidents once or twice over, and then to let them get it without book by several parts, not respecting at all whether they understand it or not. Thus they spend two or three years (for the most part) in a wearisome toile to no purpose, not knowing all the while*

what use they are to make of their book, nor what the learning of such a multitude of Rules may tend to, and *in the interim of getting the Accidents by heart* (if great care be not taken) *they loose that ability of Reading English,* which they brought from the Petty-Schoole.15

Intelligent schoolmasters like Hoole, though they saw no way to avoid the procedure itself, tried to tie the memorization process itself to data that the student knew in order to avoid "making it a work meerly for the memory, which some children are good at, though they understand nothing at all; and therefore many unskilful Masters, not knowing how to do otherwise, especially with boyes that cannot write, let them run on by rote" ("Usher's Duty," p. 34).

That Milton was well aware of these deficiencies in the educational system no doubt can exist. In one short passage in "Of Education," he condemns both the way Latin and Greek were taught and too-great emphasis on composition at too early an age:

> We do amiss to spend seven or eight years meerly in scraping together so much miserable Latine and Greek, as might be learnt otherwise easily and delightfully in one year. And that which casts our proficiency therein so much behind, is our time lost partly in . . . a preposterous exaction, forcing the empty wits of Children to compose Theams, Verses and Orations, which are the acts of ripest judgment and the final work of a head fill'd by long reading and observing, with elegant maxims, and copious invention. These are not matters to be wrung from poor striplings, like blood out of the Nose, or the plucking of untimely fruit. (CM, 4: 277–78)

That Milton's awareness of these deficiencies reflected profound dissatisfaction with his own grammar-school education is by no means so clear, however. Obviously, he had learned how to read and write Latin and Greek very well and had done outstandingly with his own early writing assignments, particularly poetry. Certainly, the verses and epistles he addressed to his former teachers, Thomas Young and Alexander Gill the Younger, attest that his respect for them continued long after his grammar-school days were over.[16]

It is likely, then, that Milton's criticism of the grammar-school curriculum did not grow out of his own experiences. Certainly, complaint about the ineffective way Latin and Greek were taught was a commonplace in the educational writings of the day.[17] It was, one might say, the seventeenth-century equivalent of the now perennial complaint that Johnny can't read; and like our modern complaint, it engendered countless solutions, none of which ever achieved widespread acceptance. In short, Milton, like most intelligent and thoughtful persons, could find much to criticize in the educational system of his day.

Whatever his reservations, however, he owed it much. His own teachers obviously avoided such excesses as allowing him to run on by rote so that he did learn Latin and Greek to the extent that when he matured, no linguistic barriers were there to hinder him in internalizing the great classical writers. If, further, he was by nature hard-working, diligent, persevering, the system certainly encouraged him in those qualities, which make themselves felt in every line he ever wrote. At its best, the system did try to instill some awareness of the moral and literary values in the writing that it taught; but even when it operated at far less than optimum capacity, it at least inculcated a mastery of language, and the importance of that for a poet cannot be over emphasized. What words can do, what they cannot do, their infinite shades of meaning, their infinite possibilities of combination, all these the unimaginative, repetitious, often cruel system taught him, and taught him well.

Musa, –ae; Musae, –arum

The word, *musa, –ae,* was the first Latin noun Milton learned to decline, being the paradigmatic first-declension noun in Lily's grammar.[18] For it, he learned a variety of meanings. Underlying them all was the Muses' attachment to the life of the mind; but as that life has many manifestations, so the

The Tender Stops of Various Quills

Muses had a variety of connotations; and eventually *musa, –ae* and the plural, *musae, –arum,* came by transference to mean things like *song, poem, studies*.[19] All these connotative and denotative differences a seventeenth-century schoolboy like Milton was expected to be as conversant with as a Roman schoolboy of the first century A.D.

Renaissance dictionaries help in establishing a basis for the possibilities of meaning that Milton knew. Representative, for example, is the entry in Thomas Cooper's *Bibliotheca Eliotae,* which was available at St. Paul's School, and does not differ significantly from those in many other works of the same period:

Musa, ae, f.g. a sweete songe.

Musae, arum, Muses, whiche were maydens, whome poetes feygned to be the daughters of Jupiter and Memorie, and that they were ladies and gouernours of poetrye and Musike. They were in numbre nine, or after some but thre. Some call them gevers of eloquence, and doo name them goddesses. It is sometime taken for poetrie or study of humanitee.

Musae mansuetiores, studies more gentill or delectable.

A musis auersus, he that hath forsaken the studye of eloquence, or that is unapte to lernynge or study.

Delectare se cum musis, to delyte hym selfe with study.[20]

Cooper, however, is merely a point of departure for understanding Milton's use of *musa, musae*. Out of all their possible meanings the one that was ultimately to be most significant for him was that of inspiratress of the divine furor that enabled the poet to write beyond the limits that rationality assigns his talents. His mastery of other meanings, however, is important too. As they work their way into his writing, they are subtle, varied, and a useful reminder of how different from our own was the idiom he learned to write.

In his own education, the first meaning he himself learned for the singular form of the word was probably "song." Other materials beside Cooper confirm this. John Brinsley, for example, who gave detailed instructions on every facet of grammar-school activity, thought that the student should

> decline perfectly every example in each Declension . . . as for example;
>
> *Musa,* a song, *musae,* of a song, *musae,* to a song, *musam* the song, *o musa,* o song, *ab hac musa* from a song, or from this song. So in the Plurall number, *musae* songs, *musarum* of songs, &c. (*Ludus Literarius,* p. 58)

By the time Brinsley gets around a page later to declining nouns and adjectives together, however, he has seemingly given it another meaning:

> As *musa bona* a good muse, *musae bonae* of a good muse, *musae bonae* to a good muse, &c. (p. 59)

If "song," then, was the first meaning that Milton learned, he learned others soon after, many of which later worked their way into his own writing.

Although he learned a little about the Muses and classical mythology in his first school years, he acquired considerably more of such material in his third year when he began to study colloquial Latin in works like Erasmus's *Colloquies* and his teachers started preparing him for more elaborate compositional efforts including versification. These more complex reading and writing assignments went hand in hand and must now be reconstructed to clarify the impact of Milton's education on his writing and attitude toward the Muses. Such reconstruction admittedly involves some speculation. My text is the Erasmian colloquy entitled "The Poetic Feast." Designed to teach schoolboys correct and idiomatic Latin through dialogue, the *Colloquies* were a staple of English grammar schools; were taught at St. Paul's later in the seventeenth century; and were, given Erasmus's prestige at that institution, almost certainly included when Milton attended as well.[21] Proof positive is lacking; but if he did not study this particular dialogue, he studied others like it and in a manner like that sketched in the following paragraphs.

All of the *Colloquies* tried to prepare students for further reading and writing through giving them generous portions of classical thought and mythology, expressed in correct and elegant phrases, ready for copying into their own paper books for use when the occasion arose. As Charles Hoole instructed:

> Let them cull out the most significant words, and phrases, and write them in a Pocket-book, with figures referring where to finde them in their Authour; and let them ever and anon be conning these by heart, because these (of all others) will stand them in most stead for speaking Latine, or writing Colloquies and Epistles. ("The Masters Method," p. 139)

Thus there was nothing accidental about the goodly number of references to the Muses that the *Colloquies* contained. They were after all a graceful and flexible legend, and there were times when references to them were absolutely the right note to sound in Latin writing or speaking. The student then was expected to note the references to the Muses and other classical figures, memorize them, classify them, and write them down for storage against the time when he would need them; and need them, sooner or later, he would.

"The Poetic Feast" opens with two characters, Hilary and Leonard, capping each others' efforts in verse, whereupon a third, Crato, exclaims: "Euge, certum est adesse Musas, effluunt carmina imprudentibus" (Bravo! Surely the muses are present: verses flow when least expected).[22] If this dialogue was taught, as with earlier reading assignments, Milton had to memorize the sentence, be prepared to state how each word in it functioned, completely decline or conjugate each word, and turn an English version of the sentence back into Erasmus's exact words if required.

Most of his teacher's efforts probably went into seeing that this kind of grammatical mastery was gained. He may, however, have devoted at least a few words to the theory of divine furor, suitably adapted to third-form ears or perhaps sent his students to the school library for further study on the matter, for the best teachers tried to work in material other than the strictly grammatical. Erasmus, for example, counselled the inclusion of biographical material, generic considerations, prosody, stylistic analysis, and moral application in teaching Terence, an author taught at about the same time in the grammar-school curriculum as the *Colloquies* and with the same end of teaching students correct and idiomatic Latin:

> You begin by offering an appreciation of the author, and state what is necessary concerning his life and surroundings, his talent, and the characteristics of his style. You next consider comedy as an example of a particular form of literature, and its interest for the student: the origin and meaning of the term itself, the varieties of Comedy, and the Terentian prosody. Now you proceed to treat briefly and clearly the argument of the play, taking each situation in due course. Side by side with this you will handle the diction of the writer; noting any conspicuous elegance, or such peculiarities as archaism, novel usage, Graecisms; bringing out anything that is involved or obscure in phrases or sentence-forms; marking, where necessary, derivations and orthography, metaphors and other rhetorical artifices. Parallel passages should next be brought under notice, similarities and contrasts in treatment observed, and direct borrowings traced. . . . The last factor in the lesson consists in the moral applications which it suggests. (Woodward, p. 174)

This, of course, was the ideal. Sometimes perhaps it even filtered down into everyday teaching. Hoole, for example, picked up and developed Erasmus's suggestions in teaching Terence; but he also wrote down the more pedestrian things that students were commonly asked to do: write out the Latin and English of their lesson in a fair hand; translate four to six lines at a time; construe the whole lesson grammatically; parse each word fully; cull out the most significant words and phrases for their pocket-books, and so on ("The Masters Method," pp. 138–41).

It is possible then that the schoolmaster gave some attention to material more appreciative and critical than grammatical in nature; and where the school had a library, it is certainly possible that he referred his students to its reference works for fuller treatment of matter like the Muses. As Hoole wrote:

> Because they [the students] must now begin to use their judgement in the right choyce of words, (when they finde many heaped together) it were not amisse to let them enquire the Original out of *Rider's* Latine *Dictionary,* or *Beckman de Originibus Latinae linguae;* and to consider the *differences* that are betwixt words of the same signification; which they may learn out of *Ausonius Popma, Laurentius Valla, Cornelius Fronto, Varro de lingua Latina,* and the like books fit to be kept in the Schoole Library. ("The Masters Method," pp. 143–44)

Some commonly used reference works provide apt glosses indeed for the passage from "The Poetic Feast." The notes to Sandys's translation of Ovid, which are representative, state "that excellent facultie and divine affection which is requisite to poetry, is not acquired by art or industry, but inspired from above.... In vaine they therefore attempt to enter at the gates of Poesy that are not rapt by the Muses." Indeed, Sandys's notes make clear that poetry not only flows *when* least expected, but among *whom* least expected; for he continues: "this gift is evident to be supernaturall, in that illiterate men not seldome prove excellent poets, expressing those arts and sciences wherein they never were instructed: in so much as when the fury is abated, they hardly understand their owne composures."[23]

Other material in "The Poetic Feast" was even more obviously directed toward steering the students toward the dictionaries and expanding their knowledge of mythology. The slatternly servant girl, Margaret, who appears in the dialogue, tells the assembled guests that when her master wants something he has all sorts of pleasant names for her—"Galatea, Euterpe, Calliope, Callirhoe, Melissa, Venus, Minerva, and I don't know what." When he is angry with her, on the other hand, she is "Tisiphone, Megara, Alecto, Medusa, Baucis, or whatever else his ill humor fancies" (Thompson, p. 161). What a golden opportunity these lists presented to send the student off to dictionaries like Cooper's *Thesaurus* where he found the following definition:

> Caliope, pes, f. g. one of the nyne Muses, whych excelled all the other in sweetenesse of voyce. Of some she is taken for the goddesse of Rhetoryke: of other for the goddesse of poetrie.[24]

Or he might have looked in Carolus Stephanus's *Dictionarium Historicum ac Poeticum,* where he would have found the following entry:

> Calliope, una Musarum, Orphei mater, quae heroico carmini praeesse existimatur, a vocis suavitate nomen habens.

> Calliope, one of the Muses, mother of Orpheus, who is deemed to preside over heroic song, having her name from the sweetness of her voice.[25]

Or he might have gone to Robertus Stephanus's *Thesaurus Linguae Latinae,* where he would have found that she was "una Musarum, & quidem praestantissima" (one of the Muses, and indeed the most illustrious one) followed by citations from Hesiod, Ovid, Virgil, Lucretius, and Martial.[26]

When Milton finished studying his text, then, he may have had some instruction as to its biographical and historical context, its literary value, its moral; but he had certainly linguistically mastered it from the ground up. He had memorized it, parsed it, studied its language carefully from every conceivable point of view, and taken that language apart and filed its components away for future use in his own writing. Writing and reading, furthermore, went hand in hand; for he was encouraged in all sorts of ways to utilize his reading assignments when he did his own prose or poetry.

As to specifics on when and how he was taught poetry writing, or more precisely versification, reconstruction is again necessary. If Aubrey's jotting is correct and Milton was a poet by the time he was ten, he probably began his instruction in verse making at home under a private tutor, Thomas Young; for as noted above, students in grammar school did not begin the preliminaries of versification until their fourth year, and Milton could hardly have established his credentials as a poet in less than a year's time doing only the simple tasks that constituted the student's first steps in writing verse. The gratitude that he expressed to Young in "Elegy 4," lines 29–32, has often been taken as indicating that Young helped him begin as a poet. If this is true, perhaps Young was less rigid in his approach than grammar-school teachers habitually were. The usual approach to the matter does, however, tell something about how he went about his business.

The customary procedure was to begin by ascertaining whether the student was able to write some Latin prose. As Brinsley stated: "Looke that they be able in good manner to write true Latine, and a good phrase in prose, before they begin to meddle with making a verse" (p. 192). Hoole is not so specific, but his placing of it in the curriculum suggests that he agreed. The next step was that they read some poetry. As Brinsley continued:

> That they have read some poetry first; as at least these bookes or the like, or some part of them: *viz. Ovid. de Tristibus,* or *de Ponto,* some piece of his Metamorphosis, or of *Virgil,* and be well acquainted with their Poeticall phrases.

Hoole was more specific as to the part of memorization in the regimen of verse writing:

> Their afternoon Lessons on Mondayes and Wednesdayes, for the first halfe year (at least) [of their fourth year] may be in *Ovids* little book *de tristibus,* wherein they may proceed by six or eight verses at a Lesson; which they should first repeat *memoriter* as perfectly as they can possibly, because the very repetition of the verses, and much more the having of them by heart, will imprint a lively pattern of Hexameters and Pentameters in their minds, and furnish them with many good *Authorities.* ("The Masters Method," pp. 156–57)

Thereafter Brinsley and Hoole somewhat diverge. Brinsley's favorite pedagogical hobbyhorse was "grammatical translation," that is, what we would call "ponies" or "cribs" as aids in teaching the student to write Latin. He felt, then, that the proper first step in teaching the student how to write Latin verse was to give him an exact word-for-word translation of Latin poetry and have him put it into Latin in English word order. Having done that, the student was then supposed to start turning the lines around one way and then another to see if he could get them into prosodically accurate lines. Let us take, for example, the first line of Ovid's *Tristia:*

> Parve—nec invideo—sine me, liber, ibis in urbem.
>
> Little book, you will go without me—and I grudge it not—to the city.[27]

Brinsley's translation would more likely have gone like this:

> Little book, you will go without me to the city, nor do I begrudge it.

He then wanted his students to translate it into Latin as follows:

> Parve liber, ibis sine me in urbem—nec invideo.

Then he encouraged them to remember what they had learned about prosody and to keep experimenting with the words until they could come up with the Ovidian order:

> Parve—nec invideo—sine me, liber, ibis in urbem.

After all, in Brinsley's view, "the making of a verse, is nothing but the turning of words forth of the Grammaticall order, into the Rhetoricall, in some kinde of metre; which we call verses," while the happy result of his approach, according to him, was the following:

> this practice of reading their Poetry, out of the translations into verse, a little triall will soone shew you, that very children will doe it as fast almost as into prose: and by the use of it, continually turning prose into verse, they will be in a good way towards the making a Verse, before they have learned any rules thereof. (p. 192)

The Tender Stops of Various Quills

Hoole's approach is a bit more to our liking, because although he too stressed the importance of the student's being able to construe, parse, and scan, he did feel that the happiest way to begin the student's career in verse writing was to have him write English verses and that the best way to begin here was to have the student actually read "some pretty delightful and honest English Poems" (pp. 157–58). Perhaps Milton's own beginning verses followed that pattern, as the phrase in *Reason of Church-Government* about "mine own choise in English, or other tongue" may suggest.

Whatever route his teachers took, however, Milton's own introduction to the writing of poetry was vastly different from ours. Perhaps his teacher held a more exalted view of versifying than its being "nothing but the turning of words forth of the Grammaticall order into the Rhetoricall, in some kinde of metre," but the fine poetic rapture described in Plato had little place in the grammar-school curriculum. Although he undoubtedly had good teachers and did his exercises well, the process for him was often, perhaps most of the time, a purely mechanical kind of thing. As such, the Muses must have meant very little indeed to him. He used them when his consultation of, say, Buchler's *Thesaurus* "for store of Epithetes, which if they bee choyse, are a singular ornament," turned up a need for them (Brinsley, p. 196). If he looked in Buchler under "Deae Fictae Liberalium Artium" [Feigned Goddesses of the Liberal Arts], he found the following list of synonyms:

> Musae, Pierides, Chorus Pierius, Camoenae, Aonides, Aoniae, Pegasides, Thespiades, Heliconiades, Helicona colentes, Heliconis alumnae, Castaliae, Maeoniae, Sicelides, Palatinae, Ascraeae, Castalides, Liberthrides, Novem Comites, Novem Sorores, Quae fontes tenent Aganippidos, Quae tenent signa equi Medusaei, Doctique cohors Heliconia Phoebi. Carminis auctores. Novena turba Aonidum sororum suggerens carmina vatibus. Habitans colens jugacelsa Montis Parnassi. Cinctae parnasside lauro. Habitantes in vertice montes Aonij. Laude Deum celebrantes, & pia facta canentes. Tertrinae sorores.

Tertres alumnae Phoebi. Sorores diae juga sacra colentes
Parnassi. Mulcentes, moventes, oblectantes animos dulcibus sonis. Flectentes, modulamine cantus. Doctae animos blandisono, dulcisono flectere canto. Nomina novem
Musarum sunt, Calliope, Clio, Erato, Thalia, Melpomene,
Terpsichore, Euterpe, Polymnia, vel Polyhymnia.[28]

His selection of the proper one was to depend on many things—on metrics of course, but also, with regard to the nexus of allusions the various phrases carried, euphony, decorum, and so on.

Because the materials about the Muses that Milton learned were extensive and varied, it would never have occurred to him that one pat definition existed for them such as today's students can find, say, in Edith Hamilton. Their main functions were to instill divine fury in the artist and to guard the intellectual life; but Milton's usage is complicated both by his employment of subsidiary meanings and of epithets like the ones just examined. Analysis of factors like these reveals how his education worked its way into his writing; underscores the strangeness, from our perspective, of the literary idiom he inherited; and makes possible a more exact reading of him.

The most complete breakdown of the different senses in which Milton used *musa, –ae; musae, –arum* has been provided by Walter MacKellar in his edition of the Latin poems. He distinguishes six different meanings: (1) a poet or poets; (2) poetic inspiration; (3) poetry; (4) a particular type of verse; (5) the arts in general; (6) the Muses in the more strictly mythological sense.[29] Elaborate as MacKellar's breakdown is, however, it could be much refined, particularly if the materials for investigation are expanded beyond the Latin poems that are his subject.

The same meanings of course are found in the English poems as in the Latin ones. Thus examples of MacKellar's first meaning of poet or poets can be found in the Latin of "Elegy 1" and the English of "Lycidas." In the former, Milton refers to Ovid as the Tarpeian Muse:

> Nec Pompeianas Tarpeia Musa columnas
> Jactet, & Ausoniis plena theatra stolis.

Let not now the Tarpeian Muse boast of Pompey's Columns, or of the theaters crowded with Ausonian stoles! (CM, 1: 172–73)

In the latter, he writes:

> So may some gentle Muse
> With lucky words favour my destin'd Urn,
> And as he passes turn,
> And bid fair peace be to my sable shrowd.[30]

Milton's use of the male pronoun, "he," shows clearly that he does not have in mind a goddess as his referent; and the sense of the passage indicates that he is using the word to denote "poet."

Not all Miltonic usage, however, can be neatly pigeonholed into one or another of MacKellar's classifications. Some, for example, mandate an additional category between poetry in general and a particular kind of verse. MacKellar's citation for the latter indicates that he uses verse in its technical sense of describing the poem's meter, and yet Milton sometimes used *muse* in the sense of a particular kind of poetry like occasional or pastoral with no reference at all to its meter.[31] An occasional, celebratory type of poetry is clearly his meaning in his letter to Alexander Gill of May 20, 1630:

> Te vero, cum prosperos sociorum successus tam sonora triumphalique tuba canere audiamus, quantum vatem sperabimus, si forte res nostrae demum feliciores tuas Musas poscant Gratulatrices.
>
> But, as we hear you sing the prosperous successes of the Allies in so sonorous and triumphal a strain, how great a poet we shall hope to have in you if by chance our own affairs, turning at last more fortunate, should demand your congratulatory muses! (CM, 12: 8–9)

On the whole, MacKellar's classifications are useful enough; and attempts to refine them are not very rewarding. It is manifestly impossible to draw the lines in such a way as completely to separate each usage from all others. The varied nature of

Muse lore, Milton's artistic subtlety, the refractory nature of language itself all preclude this.

One might think, for example, that Milton's injunction in "Lycidas," "return Sicilian Muse," fitted into the category just described, a particular kind of poetry, and that "Sicilian Muse" could be paraphrased simply as "pastoral poetry," but the matter is not that simple. The injunctive form itself indicates that some degree of personification, doubtless slight, is involved, and Milton did capitalize Muse here in the Trinity MS in contrast to his earlier phrase, "some gentle muse," where he did not. The phrase, then, partially refers to a particular type of poetry and partially to a goddess figure analogous to, if not precisely identifiable with, the Nine of Parnassus.

In short, the number of times the word *muse* appears in Milton's writings and the number of meanings he assigns to it are reflections of the education he received and tell nothing about his artistic abilities or response to the legend of the Muses. Cumulatively the references tell something about the education he received, and each such reference merits careful examination to ensure that we understand precisely what Milton was saying. For evidence of his shaping critical intelligence at work, however, examination of one particular reference in detail is necessary.

Musae Mansuetiores

I turn then to a passage in the first prolusion focusing on the phrase, *musae mansuetiores*.[32] The reader may recall its appearance in Cooper's *Bibliotheca Eliotae*. Ciceronian in origin, it was only one of many such phrases that Milton was encouraged to gather out of his reading or reference materials and then work into his own writing. Full consideration of it, how it reflects standard practices, where Milton may have gotten it, how he used it in context, relates more specifically to Milton the above comments on grammar-school education and reveals that shaping critical intellect of which I have spoken.

The grammar-school practice of encouraging students to utilize phrases from classical authors in their own work was, of course, a part of that institution's intense focus on verbal fluency in the classical languages. To this, Cambridge added other concerns, logic and metaphysics, for example; but the former focus was still emphasized so that many practices instituted in grammar school were continued in the university. This incorporation of classical phrases into the student's compositions was one of them.

On the general importance of mastering the classics, Richard Holdsworth is quite specific in his "Directions for a Student in the Universitie." A detailed course of study for undergraduates prepared by Holdsworth (1590–1649), a tutor at St. John's College and later Master of Emmanuel College, the "Directions" are not definitive in determining Milton's precise course of study, but they are suggestive. Significantly, Holdsworth wishes his undergraduates to devote their afternoon studies for all four years to mastery of Latin and Greek:

> Thus far of the Morning studies, for the first yeare. I come now to those of the afternoon for the same. Which are to be the Greek & Latine toungs History Oratory, & Poetry. Studies not less necessary than the first [that is, logic], if not more usefull, especially Latine, & Oratory, without which all the other Learning though never so eminent, is in a manner voide & useless, without those you will be bafeld in your disputes, disgraced, & vilified in Publicke examinations, laught at in speeches, & Declamations. You will never dare to appear in any act of credit in the University, nor must you look for Preferment by your Learning only. The necessity of this studie above the rest is the cause that it is to be continued through all the four yeares in the after noons . . . wheras other studies have but each a parcel of your time aloted to them.[33]

Thus Cambridge continued to emphasize the same material in much the same way that St. Paul's had. Two of the books Holdsworth recommended for study during the first year were Erasmus's *Colloquies* and Cicero's *Epistles*. To repeat, Milton probably read some of the *Colloquies* as early as his third year at St. Paul's, and there is likelihood that he read some of Cicero's *Epistles* while still in grammar school, probably around his sixth year. Similarly, Holdsworth's recommendations on how to study these materials are reminiscent of grammar-school procedure. Copying down choice phrases and idioms, Latin composition, memorizing the work studied—all these familiar practices are continued:

> Let this be your manner in reading of them; Gather out in to a paperbook all the phrases, & idiotismes which you know not allready, whether they be such as consist in single words or sentences, with the English signification and use as you goe along. This studie you may thinke teadious, but the benefit will be a sufficient requital. Spend every other afternoon, or at least two in a weeke in making latine exercises in a plain stile, for reading only without practise, will never make you a Latinist. Those may either be translations out of some plain English bookes, as Historie Dialogues Relations, or some stories, & passages which you know & have lately heard & desire to retaine, or if you will, Dialogues Epistles & Stories of your own inventing wherin you may bring in most of the usefull idiotismes which you gatherd: And so whilest you read Tully, Epistles; Stories when you read Erasmus; Dialogues when Terence. Only the first houre in every after noon must be set a part for getting without booke some Epistles in Tully, some Colloquy in Erasmus, or some Comedys in Terence. (Fletcher, 2: 638)

Now it may be that other tutors did not emphasize command of Latin as much as Holdsworth did; it may also be that Milton's tutor, Nathaniel Tovey, made allowances for his superior and well-prepared student to read different and more advanced work. No doubt can exist, however, that the cumulative effect of Milton's undergraduate training was to reenforce substantially the approach to writing that he had learned at St. Paul's. With regard to the Muses, as with all of classical mythology, the point was to note the allusions to them in one's reading and use them in one's own writing when they were apt and accorded with the over-all decorum of one's work. Something more was needed, however, for the student to achieve the highest level of incorporation that rhetorical theory taught, namely that the borrowing of such phrases redounded to the borrower's credit only when he had thoroughly assimilated his phrase to its new place and surroundings. As Quintilian had written: "A prudent man should, if he can, make his own what he sees to be best in every author."[34] This level, manifestly beyond the reach of most of his peers, is precisely the level on which to locate Milton's use of Cicero's *musae mansuetiores*.

The assignment into which he worked it, his first prolusion, was a declamation on an assigned topic, "Whether Day or Night is the more excellent," which he prepared for delivery in his own college. Milton was given the side of Day to defend, while another student took the side of Night, the entire procedure thus constituting a debate. This exercise, like other features of his college education, did not engender particularly warm feelings in his breast; but in characteristically Miltonic fashion, he designed a comprehensive strategy that enabled him at one and the same time to demonstrate his contempt for the topic and yet show off his own considerable talents. I begin, then, by analyzing his strategy, which was to treat the topic as the poetical exercise it ought to be rather than the oratorical exercise that it was; then examine what he signified with the borrowed and redirected phrase itself, namely the intellectual and artistic pursuits revealed in how he handled the exercise; and then consider his audience in terms of its varying levels of comprehension. With regard to this last point, we can legitimately posit that while a majority of his audience probably recognized the phrase, some were more familiar with it and with Milton than others; and Milton reserved the full import of his artistry for those who knew him and the phrase well.

His distaste for his assignment is revealed in his opening comment that "whether the Day is more excellent than the Night is surely no common question to dilate upon." This statement has to be taken as ironical, for the assignment of such questions was by no means uncommon, as a quick glance at any of the then current lists of debate topics reveals. John Clarke's *Quaestiones aliquot declamatoriae*, for example, listed such burning issues as "An Lucretia bene fecit, quando seipsam interfecit?" (Whether Lucretia did well when she killed herself); or, significantly for our study of "Elegy 6," "Utrum praestet *jejunare* cum Musis, quam *prandere* cum Sardanapalo?" (Whether it is better to fast with the Muses than feast with Sardanapalus?).[35]

Milton is not ironical, however, in his following statement that "this would seem more suitable for a poetical exercise than for an oratorical contest." Writers like Shakespeare had handled Lucretia's suicide very well in poetry, and Milton could not but note that his topic, while it could only awkwardly generate the severe marshaling of authority and logical proof that such assignments were supposed to generate, nevertheless had obvious poetic potential. Indeed, E. M. W. Tillyard has gone so far as to argue that "L'Allegro" is Milton's explicit rendering into poetry of the first prolusion while "Il Penseroso" is his poetic adaptation of what he planned to say were he asked to defend the opposite point of view.[36] This is going too far, of course, because there is much more in "L'Allegro" and "Il Penseroso" than poetical praise of day and night. Tillyard's work, however, is based upon a solid perception: that there is potential for poetry in Milton's topic and that his prolusion at least partially achieves that potential. Milton makes his case for the superiority of day over night not in scholastically airtight ways but rather through appealing to Greek mythology in its role as purveyor of poetic truth and through surrounding the day with as many poetic associations as possible—the birds singing at daybreak, the flowers opening their petals to the sun, and so on.

He had to develop his case, however, while still following the letter of the academic law. Thus his appeals to Greek mythology fill two functions at the same time: they poetically advance his argument, and they constitute the citations of classical authority mandatory in an academic address. In like manner, Milton conforms to, yet turns to his own end the oration's mandatory six-part structure and the incorporation into his individual sentences of the very phrasing itself of classical writers.

It is this last that is of special concern, his incorporating the Ciceronian phrase, *musae mansuetiores*, into one of his sentences, which fulfills the letter of the law but also surpasses and transforms the law through packing the phrase with such wealth of meaning as makes it genuinely functional in terms of his own individual purpose. The borrowed phrase's *locus classicus* is a celebrated epistle to Lentulus written by Cicero in 54 B.C. Though most of the letter is given over to explaining and justifying his political actions, Cicero pauses near the end, apparently in response to his friend's questioning, to recount what he himself has written of late, namely scholarly work and verse far removed in his feelings from the turbulent political arena where he must live his day-to-day existence:

> Scripsi etiam (nam ab orationibus diiungo me fere, referoque ad mansuetiores Musas, quae me maxime, sicut iam a prima adolescentia, delectant); scripsi igitur Aristoteleo more, quemadmodum quidem volui, tres libros in disputatione ac dialogo *De Oratore*, quos arbitror Lentulo tuo fore non inutiles. Abhorrent enim a communibus praeceptis, atque omnem antiquorum et Aristoteleam et Isocrateam rationem oratoriam complectuntur. Scripsi etiam versibus tres libros *De Temporibus Meis*.

> I have also written (you see I am more or less disengaging myself from the lure of oratory and returning to the gentler Muses, who are now, as they ever have been from my earliest youth, my chief delight), I have written, I say, on the model of Aristotle—at least that is how I wanted to do it—three books in the form of a discussion and dialogue, entitled *The Orator*, which I think will be of some use to your son Lentulus; for they disagree entirely with the commonly accepted rules, and embrace all the theories of rhetoric held by the ancients, including those of Aristotle and Isocrates. Furthermore, I have written three books in verse on *My Own Times*.[37]

Milton worked the phrase *musae mansuetiores* into the end of a long passage of dilation on the many splendors of the day, which he rounded out by assuring his listeners that they could find confirmation within themselves for what he had established from without:

> Vos testor, Academici, quam jucundum, quam optatum diuque expectatum vobis illucescat mane, utpote quod vos

ad mansuetiores Musas revocet, a quibus insaturabiles & sitibundos dimiserat ingrata nox.

I call you to witness, fellow students, what a joyous, what a delightful daily expectation dawns upon you in the morning, seeing that it summons you again to the more gentle Muses, from whom the disagreeable night has separated you, insatiable and thirsty. (CM, 12: 138–39)

From our own decadent modern perspective, we tend to view this as irony; and doubtless there were those among Milton's listeners who hated to get up early and harbored some such thought as the following: "How many more mornings am I going to have to get up to listen to junk like this?" Such students very possibly greeted the phrase with just the "grins, and maybe a few good-natured jeers" that William Riley Parker has posited (*Milton*, vol. 1, p. 108). Others, however, who could situate the phrase in its context and who knew Milton personally, found in it a deeper and more beautiful meaning; for these gentler Muses were the guardians of the poetry and learning that Milton was deeply attached to, that he managed to work into a not particularly promising assignment, and that he found in kindred spirits at Cambridge, if not in Cambridge's curriculum.

These kindred spirits were, of course, interspersed among others less kindred in Milton's audience; but a consideration of the varying degrees of comprehension possible within a Christ's College convocation establishes that Milton, though painstakingly craftsmanlike in his use of the phrase, had no reason to feel that his usage was too learned for a majority of his listeners to grasp. To be sure, there were the uneducated, the unintelligent, and the unmotivated; but they were not his concern. Among the rest, while perceptions of Milton's artistry varied according to whether the person had read Cicero recently or long ago or whether he had encountered the gentler Muses in Cicero himself or in one of the thesauri of the day, the evidence is considerable that most could at least recognize the phrase as Ciceronian.

The practice of teaching at least some of Cicero's epistles in grammar school was widespread. T. W. Baldwin, in his comprehensive survey of sixteenth-century curricula, adduces proof that they were taught at Bangor, Harrow, Norwich, East Retford, Tideswell, Guisborough, Eton, and Westminster.[38] Adam Martindale shows that they were taught even in not very illustrious schools like the Free School of St. Helen's that he attended.[39] With regard to St. Paul's itself, Donald Lemen Clark in his conjectured curriculum for the school during Milton's day has speculated that some of them at least were taught in the sixth year there.[40]

Less certainty attends whether this particular letter was taught, of course. Most schoolmasters probably used only portions of them. As the statutes at Guisborough recommended: "Tullies epistles or so many of them as he [the schoolmaster] shall thinke fit for the capacitie & profit of his schollars in the same . . ." (*Small Latine,* 1: 431). Some of the more energetic ones like Charles Hoole, however, recommended that "the Scholars in the upper Forms . . . imploy themselves in perusal of all *Tullies* Epistles" ("The Masters Method," p. 155). It would not be extraordinary, then, for his peers to have read this letter during their grammar-school days; but if they did not, Holdsworth's "Directions," quoted above, make clear that they could well have read (or reread) the letter as a part of assigned work during their first year at Cambridge.

On the other hand, they need not have read the letter at all in order to recognize the phrase, for it was cited in numerous reference works including two that appear in early lists of books at St. Paul's: Cooper's *Thesaurus,* already quoted, and the far more comprehensive work of Robertus Stephanus (Robert Estienne). Stephanus's *Thesaurus Linguae Latinae* not only summarized much encyclopedic material about the Muses, but also gave, with comment, copious citations for various uses. Here is his relevant entry:

> Mansuetiores. Cic. Lentulo, libro I.9, Ab oratoribus diiungo me fere, referoque ad mansuetiores musas. Id est philosophicas disputationes. Mansuetiores musas est qui versus interpretetur: alius dialogos, & huiusmodi scripta, in quibus non requiritur orationum grauitas.

Mansuetiores. Cicero to Lentulus, Book I, Letter 9. I am separating myself more or less from orations and returning to the gentler muses. That is to philosophical disputations. That is how the line translates "mansuetiores musas": another possibility is dialogues and writings of the sort in which the seriousness of orations is not required.

Consultation of these reference works further enhances an appreciation of how Milton traded on normative definitions in creating fresh work. Cooper, for example, defined the gentler Muses as "more pleasant and delectable studies, that most refreshe the wit, as poetrie, histories, etc." In other words, they were studies like those that Milton most enjoyed and often criticized Cambridge for not providing. Even more precisely did Stephanus's definition, "dialogues and writings of the sort in which the seriousness of orations is not required," underscore what I have said was Milton's over-all strategy for his oration.

The full import of his usage, however, was reserved for those who could place the phrase in its original Ciceronian context and relate their understanding of it to a personal knowledge of Milton himself. He uses the words exactly as they appeared in Cicero, *mansuetiores Musas,* and trades upon sentiments present in Cicero but left out of the reference works. Even the comprehensive Stephanus had omitted from his quotation the phrase following "the gentler Muses," where Cicero provides the additional information that these Muses "are now, as they ever have been from my earliest youth, my chief delight." Those in his audience who knew Milton himself—and this prolusion was prepared for presentation in the college where everyone more or less knew everyone else— would have no problem in applying Cicero's words to the young speech maker. For Milton, no less than Cicero, the gentler Muses had been from earliest youth his chief delight, as he and those who knew him were to assert again and again.

Just as familiarity with Milton's interests and habits enriched his listeners' delight in his allusion, so was that delight similarly heightened by familiarity with the extended passage in Cicero; for Cicero's details of what he has written under the aegis of the gentler Muses relate closely to Milton's own efforts: "three books . . . of discussion and dialogue . . . which . . . disagree entirely with the commonly accepted rules, and embrace all the theories of rhetoric held by the ancients . . . [and] three books in verse." In applying these details to Milton himself, listeners understood that Milton was not trying to establish one-to-one correspondences between his fifteen-page prolusion and Cicero's three carefully crafted books of rhetorical theory, nor between his poetry and Cicero's. Those listening carefully, however, might well see that Milton's little prolusion, slight though it was, shared the same goal as Cicero's massive achievement: to demonstrate that the rules now commonly accepted were inadequate and that a return, in an innovative spirit, to older and more illustrious models, would create a more distinguished discourse. And they might also see that the composing of verse was for him, as it had been for Cicero, a release from the tedium of daily duty. If, finally, they had read or heard any of Milton's poetic efforts, they realized that this last point of comparison worked to Milton's advantage rather than Cicero's; for Cicero, though a superb prose stylist, was a poor poet.

The careful listeners who knew their Cicero and their Milton were not thus apt to greet Milton's description of the dawn summoning them to the gentler Muses with "grins, and maybe a few good-natured jeers" whether their biorhythms agreed or not. However much they may have disliked getting out of bed of a morning, this feeling was outweighed by their awareness that the gentler Muses invoked by the speaker, though often difficult to perceive in the daily grind of academic life, were never far afield for those who truly loved literature and philosophy. These listeners may not have cared much for Milton as a person; they may have felt, as many subsequently have, that he was a bit too insistent upon his own merits. They could not but be impressed, however, by the gracefulness of allusion with which he bound them to himself as fellow-citizens in an ancient but still flourishing republic of letters.

The Mellowing Year

MILTON'S USE of *musae mansuetiores*, though a slight thing in comparison with his creation of Urania, exhibits no less than that creation his hallmark of personalizing inherited materials. Two poems, "Elegy 6" and the Nativity Ode, demonstrate his growing ability to incorporate many writers and varied traditions into his own ideas about and experience of inspiration. Written in the scholastic and supposedly impersonal medium of Latin verse, "Elegy 6" furnishes an effective transition between work written to fulfill external requirements and poetry written to fulfill inner ones. Of the latter sort, the Nativity Ode is Milton's first major achievement. Discussion of its stanzas dealing with inspiration thus serves as a fitting prelude to a discussion of *Paradise Lost*.

The Nativity Ode's significance for Milton is attested by his pulling it out of chronological order and placing it first in his *Poems* published in 1645. For him, obviously, the Nativity Ode represented his poetic coming of age. Written in English and invoking for the first time the Heavenly Muse, the stanzas having to do with inspiration unobtrusively blend the elements of his mature art: the classical, the Christian, the personal; and they do so under the aegis, or so Milton believed, of a force beyond himself. It is a work of genius, and its creation involves psychological processes not yet well understood. For Milton, the matter was simple: God was the ultimate Author of this work, and he merely the conduit through which it came into the world. Or, to use his blending of classical and Christian, the Heav'nly Muse spoke, and he listened:

> Say Heav'nly Muse, shall not thy sacred vein
> Afford a Present to the Infant God?
> Hast thou no verse, no hymn, or solemn strein,
> To welcome him to this his new abode,
> Now while the Heav'n by the Suns team untrod,
>   Hath took no print of the approaching light,
> And all the spangled host keep watch in squadrons
>   bright?
>
> See how from far upon the Eastern rode
> The Star-led Wisards haste with odours sweet,
> O run, prevent them with thy humble ode,
> And lay it lowly at his blessed feet;
> Have thou the honour first, thy Lord to greet,
>   And joyn thy voice unto the Angel Quire,
> From out his secret Altar toucht with hallow'd fire.
>   (CM, 1: 1–2)

The Muse obviously had much to teach him, but family, education, religion, character, and culture all conspired to make him a slow pupil in her school. Earnestness, thoroughness of preparation, a willingness to work long hours, these were so much a part of Milton that it took many years and much more experience of the creative process, positive and negative, before he finally internalized and accepted the lesson of the Nativity Ode, that one can prepare for writing great poetry through reading, study, and practice of one's style, but that the creation of art itself cannot be called up at will. To Milton's lifelong struggle with this principle and his final liberating acceptance of it I shall turn in Chapter 4.

Your Muse; My Camena

In "Elegy 6," inspiration and the composition of poetry constitute the poem's subject matter. In a sense, then, the poem is more revelatory of Milton's thoughts on those matters than the stanzas in the Nativity Ode. Those stanzas, after all, imply attitudes, but do not state them. "Elegy 6," by contrast, makes definite statements: this kind of poetry grows out of this kind of inspiration; that kind of poetry, out of quite different inspiration. Thus reduced to its skeletal minimum, the poem promises to be revealing; and fleshed out in the manner Milton decided upon, it is revealing not only of Milton's views on the prerequisites for different kinds of poetry, but also of such issues as his training and its effect on his writing. This is due to the circumstances of its composition, which place it far more in line with the verse making it was assumed all educated gentlemen could do, so that it reflects Milton's education and training in a more direct way than the Nativity Ode does.

The title and headnote give the poem's background:

Ad Carolum Diodatum ruri commorantem.
Qui cum idibus Decemb. scripsisset, & sua carmina excusari postulasset si solito minus essent bona, quod inter lautitias quibus erat ab amicis exceptus, haud satis felicem operam Musis dare se posse affirmabat, hunc habuit responsum.

To Charles Diodati, the While He Tarried in the Country. When Diodati had written, on the Ides of December, asking that, if his verses should be less good than usual, their shortcomings should be forgiven, because, so he affirmed, amid the splendid entertainments wherewith he had been greeted by his friends he had not been able to give to the Muses auspicious services, he had this answer. (CM, 1: 206–207)

In the poem itself, Milton indicates Diodati had asked him to reply in verse (lines 3–4), so "Elegy 6," unlike the Nativity Ode, wells up from no deep inner compulsion and, not surprisingly, draws more obviously on what he had learned in school. "The making of verses"; the figures like the Muses, the Camenae, Thalia, Erato; the historical figures like Homer; the debate techniques that required preparation on both sides of an issue—all these he incorporates into his reply.

The process whereby he organized these elements into a

poem can plausibly be reconstructed. Since Diodati had said that his own verse was not very good, politeness mandated that Milton reply something like "Your poetry is not so bad. Actually it's rather good." Since Diodati had further specified that the reason his poetry was not up to his usual standards was because of the lavish wining and dining his friends had accorded him, what more natural than that Milton add a few exempla to show that wining and dining are actually aids in writing a certain kind of poetry? The remainder of the poem, the contrast with another kind of poetry that grows out of abstemious living, is not so inevitable, but the lines both personal and academic along which Milton's mind proceeded are easy enough to follow. Diodati had already suggested a contrast between his own carefree disposition and Milton's more studious one.

> Why inexcusably persist in hanging over books and studies all day and all night? Live, laugh make the most of youth and the hours; and cease studying the zeals and recreations and indolences of the wise men of old, wearing yourself out the while. I, in all things else inferior to you, in this one thing, in knowing when to set a measure to my labors, both seem to myself, and am, your better. Farewell and be joyous—though not in the fashion of Sardanapalus in Cilicia. (CM, 12: 295)

Given Milton's education, the development of this contrast was, literally, child's play. The emphasis on debate had ensured that. Having centered roughly one-half of his poem around the figure of the wine-drinking love poet, he easily finished it out with a contrasting figure, the water-drinking poet whose subject matter is the serious and sublime.

In developing both figures, he had all sorts of materials at hand. He may already have partially organized them in preparation for some debate or oration in which he had to participate. Some of the common topics for debate listed in manuals of the day conceivably could lead to results somewhat like "Elegy 6." One of John Clarke's *Quaestiones aliquot declamatoriae* was "Utrum praestet *jejunare* cum Musis, quam *prandere* cum Sardanapalo?" (Whether it is better to fast with the Muses or feast with Sardanapalus).¹ Doubtless, Milton felt that little enough could be said for feasting with this effeminate Persian king whose very name had become a symbol of luxurious depravity; but like all debaters, he had to come to terms with topics where all the best points seemingly were ranged on one side. One solution, obviously, was to palliate the worse side, to grant, for example, that eating and drinking and merrymaking had gotten a bad press but were not really so bad as they had been portrayed, had even in some instances perhaps given rise to good things, like a certain kind of poetry not to be despised.

Whether or not Milton worked up such material on his own, however, the contrast of wine- and water-drinking as they impinged on poetic composition was encountered at every turn and given every conceivable development possible. Scaliger, Minturno, Spenser, Herrick, Comes, John Eliot, Owen Felltham had all written on it as Zera S. Fink documented nearly fifty years ago.² Ample as Fink's list was, it could have been expanded and illuminated by consideration of how authors altered the *topos* in terms of their current literary need. Alexander Ross's *Mystagogus Poeticus,* though too late to be a source for "Elegy 6," is useful in its modest, handbook sort of way as a summation of what "everyone" more or less knew about the topic:

> the Muses were called Nymphes, and because they drunke Water rather then Wine: Notwithstanding *Horace* speakes against Water-drinkers, that they cannot be good Poets: He loved Wine and Wenching too well, to believe his commendation of either: a farre better Poet then he, who was called the Virgin Poet, both for his temperance and abstinence, was no Winebibber; I finde that wine in some dull and Phlegmatick bodies, may a little helpe the invention, yet doubtlesse it is an enemy to judgement, which is most of all required in a Poet.³

This was the norm, the kind of book that Richard Holdsworth recommended to his students to brush up on before tackling Ovid's *Metamorphoses:* "Before you read Ovids' Metamorphosis it will be requisite to run over some book of Mythology. Natalis

Comes is somewhat too large, & tedious Sr Francis Bacon too short I direct you to this as most convenient" (Fletcher, 2: 639). Individual writers were able to give the norm a different flavor depending on the purpose of the passage they were writing at the moment. Ben Jonson, for example, not surprisingly found wine vastly superior to water as a means of poetic inspiration in lines meant to be set "Over the Door at the Entrance into the Apollo" and consequently downgraded the Muses as silly girls of no account:

> He the half of Life abuses,
> That sits watering with the Muses.
> Those dull Girls no good can mean us,
> Wine, it is the Milk of Venus,
> And the Poet's Horse accounted:
> Ply it, and you all are mounted.[4]

Milton, characteristically, took the matter in yet another direction. In order to develop his contrast, he seized first on the portion of the tradition adumbrated in Ross's phrase, "Horace speaks against Water-drinkers, that they cannot be good Poets." His strategy is to demonstrate that the Muses, regardless of what his readers think they know about them, really have all sorts of associations with wine. Thus, in lines 21–22, he alludes to Anacreon's charming celebrations of wine and love:

> Quid nisi vina, rosaque racemiferumque Lyaeum
>   Cantavit brevibus Teia Musa modis?

> Of what save wines, and roses, and cluster-bearing Lyaeus
> did the Teian Muse sing in her [or his] short measures?
> (CM 1: 208–209)

If the name of poetry is not to be denied such exquisite work, then surely, Milton implies, it is foolish to deny that connections exist between the Muses and wine.

In carrying out his strategy, Milton's vocabulary everywhere demonstrates how closely attached this poem is to his academic training. His use of Muse in its associative meaning of poet, for example, ties his comment about Anacreón (the Teian

Muse) closely to the general point it is meant to illustrate. Other examples are contained in lines 17–18, which state that "again and yet again on the Aonian Hills the nine-fold throng, mingling with the Thyonean troop, has cried aloud, *Euoe!*"

> Saepius Aoniis clamavit collibus Euoe
> Mista Thyoneo turba novena choro.
>   (CM, 1: 208–209)

The phrases, "nine-fold throng" and "Thyonean troop," demonstrate Milton's awareness, ground in through years of training, that "Epithetes, if they bee choyse, are a singular ornament." "Thyonean troop" (*Thyoneo choro*) was an epithet for Bacchic devotees, depending on Thyone, an alternate name for Semele, Bacchus's mother, for its association; "nine-fold throng" (*turba novena*), a frequently encountered epithet for the Muses. It appears, for example, in the list from Buchler quoted in Chapter 2.

Thus Milton sought to convince Diodati that regardless of what he had read in his handbooks, the Muses really did have all sorts of connections with wine. Having so connected them, however, he then needed a contrasting set of deities to preside over the abstemious life and noble poetry he described in the second portion of the poem. He found them in the Camenae, Roman goddesses who had long been identified with the Muses. Addressing Diodati, he writes:

> At tua quid nostram prolectat Musa camoenam,
> Nec sinit optatas posse sequi tenebras?

But why does *your* Muse seek to lure forth *mine*? Why does your Muse not suffer mine to court the obscurity she craves? (CM, 1: 206–207)

To make clear what Milton is saying, I should, instead of italicizing *your* and *mine*, stick with the different words he uses:

> Why does your *Muse* seek to lure forth my *Camena*?

This clarifies Milton's discriminations, but only if they are studied against the background of his education. In order to understand the subtle and original meaning that informs all his allusions to these deities, we need to understand both the norms and Milton's departure from them. The Camenae served Milton's purposes so well because he had thoroughly mastered Hoole's instructions in developing his own "judgement in the right choyce of words" and indeed had now gone so far beyond these instructions that none of the dictionaries or thesauri provided clear-cut precedent for his usage.

The word *camena* was Latin in origin and appeared many times in Latin authors.[5] Early identified with the Muses, the Camenae always appeared in any list of synonyms for them; nor were they sharply differentiated from them. Milton's own usage always connotes a certain simplicity in its referent; but as the word *simplicity* itself suggests different meanings, so do Milton's Camenae. The response to *simplicity* depends on its frame of reference. Thus we deprecate an artless ditty by calling it simple in comparison to a complex masterpiece; we do not, however, deprecate country life by calling it simple in comparing it to the hectic pace of the city. As Roman goddesses, the Camenae lent themselves to both frames of reference. When differentiated from the Muses, they could suggest a certain simplicity that was a defect if rudely simple Latin letters were compared with the sophisticated Greek; a virtue if the plain life of the Republic were compared to the Asiatic luxury of the Empire.

They appear in four other of his poems beside "Elegy 6": "To His Father," "To Salsilli," "Manso," and "Epitaph for Damon." The simplicity of reference is deprecating in "To His Father," "To Salsilli," and "Manso," but not in "Epitaph for Damon" or "Elegy 6." In "To His Father," line 7, for example, Milton takes the stance that his verse up to now has not been particularly good, but he maintains the greatness of poetry and the possibility of his attaining to such greatness. When writing of the latter two, he uses *Musa;* when writing of the first, *Camoena.* Thus in line 5, he urges his inspirational spirit to "rise on daring pinions," using *Musa;* and in line 56 he rounds out a long passage on the greatness of poetry with a prayer to his father not "to hold cheap the holy Muses":

Nec tu perge precor sacras contemnere Musas.

But when he refers to his father's pretended dislike of his poetic efforts to date, he uses *camoenas* as a way of indicating that perhaps his work has not been as outstanding as it might have been:

> Tu tamen ut simules teneras odisse camoenas,
> Non odisse reor, neque enim, pater, ire jubebas
> Qua via lata patet, qua pronior area lucri,
> Certaque condendi fulget spes aurea nummi.

Though you pretend that you loathe the dainty Camenae, none the less you loathe them not, methinks, for, father, you did not bid me go where a highway lies open wide and broad, where the ground slopes more straightly to gain, and the golden hope of storing away money shines with steady luster. (CM, 1: 274–75)

During his sojourn in Italy, particularly aware of his cultural disadvantages as a Northerner, he used the Camenae in two poems to suggest the inadequacy of his work. In "To Salsilli," addressed to an Italian poet who had praised Milton's work extravagantly, Milton indicates that the praise was undeserved, labelling his Muse "nostra camoena":

> haec s'is verba pauca Salsillo
> Refer, camoena nostra cui tantum est cordi,
> Quamque ille magnis praetulit immerito divis.

bear, if you will, these few words to Salsilli, who takes our Camena so warmly to his heart, preferring her—undeservedly—to the truly mighty poets. (CM, 1: 282–83)

Similar deprecation of his work appears in the opening lines of "Manso," where Milton wonders whether the power of his song is sufficient to elevate the Marquis of Manso to the poetic prominence he deserves.

> Tu quoque si nostrae tantum valet aura Camoenae,
> Victrices hederas inter, laurosque sedebis.

You too, if the breath of our Camena has power so great, shall have a seat among the victors' crowns of ivy and of laurel. (CM, 1: 286–87)

This modesty is in keeping with his awareness of his inexperience as a poet and of the relatively low status of English as opposed to Italian culture, although his stance modulates in the poem's later portions where he finds the material of Britain not inappropriate as subject matter of his projected epic.

In "Epitaph for Damon" and "Elegy 6," however, no deprecation is intended. In "Epitaph for Damon," he hopes that the "aid of native Muses" *(patriis camoenis)* will help him to "sound forth a truly British strain."[6] As in "Elegy 6" he dispassionately presents the advantages of two quite different kinds of poetry, so in "Epitaph for Damon," he notes without rancor that dedicating himself to a British subject in the British tongue will mean foregoing fame beyond the limits of his own country. In both "Manso" and "Epitaph for Damon," Milton is in a sense willing to admit the superiority of Latin culture and language, but only in a sense, and his preference in these contexts for the Camenae is instructive. As the Latins admired the superiority of Greek art and literature, yet found something superior in their own simple and dignified heritage, so Milton could pay homage to his Italian friends' heritage yet maintain that his native tradition embodied positive values worthy of epic celebration. In such contexts, the Camenae, with their Latin associations, were a better word choice than the Muses.

Indeed, the Latinity of the Camenae was the most obvious reason for his selecting them as his tutelary deities in opposition to Diodati's. Diodati's verses, like his surviving letters, may have been written in Greek so that "in juxtaposing Diodati's Greek *Musa* . . . with *nostram camoenam,* Milton may be not merely using a variant term but modestly deprecating his own verses" (*Var. Comm.,* 1: 115). And yet it is "deprecation" only in a sense. That something of the Romans' mixed attitude toward the Greeks comes through in Milton's praise of Diodati's work is suggested by other factors that made them apt for his purposes: their association with a specific Roman spring; the commonly accepted etymology of their name; and their carrying as connotations both the rude simplicity and the plain dignity that early Rome was thought to have possessed. Although the reference works of Milton's day were not so clear on the matter as today's, he could by collating his reading of classical authors such as Livy, Juvenal, and Vitruvius, associate the Camenae with a certain Roman spring that in historical times had been given to the Vestal Virgins.[7] This had been done by Numa, the legendary second king of Rome, a man, Livy tells us, whose "training was not in foreign studies, but in the stern and austere discipline of the ancient Sabines, a race incorruptible as any race of the olden time" ("non tam peregrinis artibus quam disciplina tetrica ac tristi veterum Sabinorum, quo genere nullum quondam incorruptius fuit").[8] Livy's mention of the spring and its dedication to the Camenae occurs, furthermore, in a passage expounding on how Numa so imbued the ancient Romans with reverence for the gods that they became law abiding and peace loving, while their neighbors "came to feel such reverence for them, that they thought it sacrilege to injure a nation so wholly bent upon the worship of the gods." He continues:

> There was a grove watered by a perennial spring which flowed through the midst of it, out of a dark cave. Thither Numa would often withdraw, without witnesses, as if to meet the goddess; so he dedicated the grove to the Camenae.
>
> Et cum ipsi se homines in regis velut unici exempli mores formarent, tum finitimi etiam populi, qui antea castra, non urbem positam in medio ad sollicitandam omnium pacem crediderant, in eam verecundiam adducti sunt ut civitatem totam in cultum versam deorum violare ducerent nefas. Lucus erat, quem medium ex opaco specu fons perenni rigabat aqua. Quo quia se persaepe Numa sine arbitris velut ad congressum deae inferebat, Camenis eum lucum sacravit. (1: 72–75)

The Camenae, then, were associated with an heroic period in Roman history; with a king who had owed his virtues not to foreign learning, but to the austere mores of the ancient people to whom he belonged; and with the Vestal Virgins whose pledge of perpetual chastity amplified the goddesses' aura of antiquity, severity, and piety.

In his third satire, Juvenal, naturally enough, dwelled on the debased state of their spring in his day:

> Hic, ubi nocturnae Numa constituebat amicae,
> nunc sacri fontis nemus et delubra locantur
> Iudaeis, quorum cophinus faenumque supellex
> (omnis enim populo mercedem pendere iussa est
> arbor et eiectis mendicat silva Camenis).
> in vallem Egeriae descendimus et speluncas
> dissimiles veris. quanto praesentius esset
> numen aquis, viridi si margine clauderet undas
> herba, nec ingenuum violaret marmora tofum.

Here Numa held his nightly assignations with his mistress; but now the holy fount and grove and shrine are let out to Jews, who possess a basket and a truss of hay for all their furnishings. For as every tree nowadays has to pay toll to the people, the Camenae have been ejected, and the wood has to go a-begging. We go down to the Valley of Egeria, and into the caves so unlike to nature: how much more near to us would be the spirit of the fountain if its waters were fringed by a green border of grass, and there were no marble to outrage the native tufa![9]

Further evidence for identifying the Camenae with this particular spring was to be found in Vitruvius's *On Architecture:*

> Sunt autem etiam nonnulli fontes calidi, ex quibus profluit aqua sapore optimo, quae in potione ita est suavis, uti nec fontalis ab Camenis nec Marcia saliens desideretur.

> There are some hot springs from which water flows of excellent flavour and so pleasant to drink that we miss neither the Fountain of the Camenae nor the conduit of the Marcian Aqueduct.[10]

Their indigenous characteristic was thus very much a factor in Latin references to the Camenae, this native quality acquiring added luster in the days of Empire from the idealized vision of early Roman history that prevailed.

That they had a certain numinous quality might be intuited from Livy, but actually there was much more of an aura of the holy about them than one would gather first from reading him. Their name the Romans had derived from *carmen*, which means not only *song* in Latin, but also *oracular response, prophecy, incantation*. The linguistic transformation of casmena > carmena > camena was given in Varro's *On the Latin Language* and still accepted in Milton's day. Significantly, the quotations from ancient Latin poetry that Varro gives amplify precisely the qualities of antiquity and sacredness that Milton wishes to work into his own poem:

> Quare e Casmena Carmena, [e] Carmena R extrito Camena factum. Ab eadem voce canite, pro quo in Saliari versu scriptum est cante, hoc versu:
> Divum em pa cante, divum deo supplicate.
> In Carmine Priami quod est:
> Veteres Casmenas cascam rem volo profarier.
>
> Therefore from *Casmena* came *Carmena,* and from *Carmena,* with loss of the R, came *Camena*. From the same radical came *canite* 'sing ye,' for which in a Salian verse is written *cante,* and this is the verse:
> Sing ye to the Father of the Gods, entreat the God of Gods.
> In *The Song of Priam* there is the following:
> I wish the ancient Camenae to tell a story old.[11]

For Milton, Varro's derivations survived not only in Varro, but in Renaissance reference works like Carolus Stephanus's *Dictionarium Historicum ac Poeticum:*

> Camoenae, eadem quae Musae, Iovis & Memoriae filiae, a cantus amoenitate (vt quidam volunt) ita appelatae. Varro tamen author est, ab antiquis Carmoenas & Casmoenas dictas fuisse, quae postea abiecto r vel s, Camoenae sunt appellatae.
>
> Camenae, which are the same as the Muses, the daughters of Jupiter and Memory, are so called from the loveliness of song (as some are of the opinion). Varro still is the au-

thority for their having been called Carmenae and Casmenae by the ancients; who thereafter, by throwing away the *r* or *s* were called Camenae.[12]

With their name, then, went some of the associations of magic and power that the word, *carmen,* could carry. Sometimes, it is true, the word merely meant *song.* At other times, however, it clearly carried a far more potent meaning, as in the Virgilian line "carminibus Circe socios mutavit Ulixi" (the charms with which Circe transformed the companions of Ulysses), or the Horatian *libros carminum,* "the books of incantations that have power to unfix the stars and call them down from heaven."[13] With such quotations in mind, perhaps, Robertus Stephanus wrote of the Camenae:

> a carminibus sunt dictae, vel quod canunt antiquorum laudes, vel quod sunt castae metis praesides
>
> they are named from song, either because they sing the praises of ancient times or because they are the chaste guardians of wisdom.[14]

Furthermore, since the nature of such works was to reproduce what had appeared in countless other similar works, Milton would have read similar material had he never been exposed to either Carolus or Robertus Stephanus.

From these works and others like them, we may conclude that the Camenae for Milton carried associations of the dignity and simplicity that early Rome possessed and also the power that poetry in its loftiest reaches could convey. In claiming them as his patronesses, he is deprecating his verses in the sense that a Roman might deprecate his native heritage in comparing it with the Greek. The Romans on the one hand admired the richness of Greek culture and language, as in Cicero's off-handed reference to "our Greek friends, whose language is richer [copiosior] than ours."[15] On the other hand, they felt that Greek luxury had been a debilitating influence on the virtues of the Republic. Thus Juvenal looked to the Greek cities of Sybaris, Rhodes, Miletus, and Tarentum as the sources of the love-making, feasting, and drinking that stained the Roman scene. It was poverty and hardship, he wrote, that had formerly kept Latium virtuous. Now, however, he saw that virtue destroyed by "the calamities of long peace [and] Luxury more deadly than any foe":

> nullum crimen abest facinusque libidinis, ex quo
> paupertas Romana perit. hinc fluxit ad istos
> et Sybaris colles, hinc et Rhodos et Miletos
> atque coronatum et petulans madidumque Tarentum.

Since the day when Roman poverty perished, no deed of crime or lust has been wanting to us; from that moment Sybaris and Rhodes and Miletus have poured in upon our hills, with the begarlanded and drunken and unabashed Tarentum.[16]

Though developed with greater asperity, Juvenal's contrast of Republic and Empire involves the same opposites presented by Milton in "Elegy 6." In the light of Juvenal and the other Latin writers quoted, it is clear that the Camenae were appropriate inspiratresses for the poet who Milton says must "let pellucid water stand near him, in a tiny cup of beechen wood, and . . . drink only sober draughts from a pure spring," a poet who must also lead "a youth free of crime, pure, and chaste." As for that poet's further character as an "augur . . . resplendent with holy vestments and with lustral waters," the etymologies that Milton read in Varro, in Carolus Stephanus, and in Robertus Stephanus made connections with the Camenae eminently appropriate. If, as Robertus Stephanus wrote, the Camenae "are named from song, either because they sing the praises of ancient times or because they are the chaste guardians of wisdom," then they easily attached themselves to the poet Milton described in lines 55–78 and to the figures he mentioned as worthy of emulation, prophets like Tiresias and Calchas, singers of literally enchanting song like Linus and Orpheus, praisers of ancient times like Homer. They embodied that "condition of complete simplicity" T. S. Eliot described as "costing not less than everything"—the simplicity achieved when all that is frivolous and extraneous to high purpose has been stripped from life and art.

Once again, there was nothing inevitable about Milton's

using the Camenae as he did. For many of the classical writers, the Camenae and Muses were simply interchangeable. Perhaps because he was writing in Greek, Plutarch, when he recounted the story of Numa and the spring's dedication, referred to the goddesses as Muses.[17] On the other hand, the Old Latin poet, Livius Andronicus, (third century, B.C.) substituted the Camenae for the Muses in his adaptation of Homer's *Odyssey* so that the poem's first line became "Virum mihi, Camena, insece versutum."[18] Varro identified them with the Muses (1: 292–93); and this same attitude prevailed among the Renaissance Latinists as well. Carolus Stephanus, for example, explicitly stated that the Camenae "are the same as the Muses." In like fashion, Thomas Cooper's *Thesaurus* defined Camena briefly as "one of the ix muses, a songe."[19]

It was therefore from scattered and inconclusive materials that Milton created a meaning for the Camenae eminently appropriate to the passages in which he used them. Appreciation of what he had done, in his own day as now, depended on a steeping in the same materials he had steeped himself in. A reader like Diodati, trained in the same school as Milton, could readily appreciate what he had done without stopping to refresh his memory by thumbing through the nearest thesaurus. His response was perhaps only a slight pause to savor this familiar yet novel usage. It is difficult for us to approximate the same response because the very laboriousness with which we have to reconstruct its background causes us perhaps overly to exaggerate Milton's achievement here; and yet surely an educated seventeenth-century response involved some recognition, even if subliminal, that his usage was recognizable and yet superior to what prior usage led one to anticipate.

"Elegy 6," then, shows Milton skillfully using the Muse lore he had learned in school. More than that, however, it shows him using the materials mastered there to write about himself and to incorporate into them the Christian element so important to him. That the poem includes autobiographical elements, especially in its portrait of the serious poet, has not been unanimously accepted. William Riley Parker, for example, argued that Milton was merely developing two sides of a debate topic without committing himself to either.[20] The consensus of critical opinion from David Masson to Anthony Low, however, has been that that portion of the poem was autobiographical; was, in Douglas Bush's words, "a statement none the less deeply felt for being put—like the theme of Lycidas—in oblique and impersonal terms."[21]

Indeed, the poem as a whole, for all its being expressed "in oblique and impersonal terms," tells much about Milton's circumstances and attitudes in writing it. That he may have altered some of the facts to heighten artistic effects no longer needs stressing; that the artistic effects, so far as we can tell, accord with the facts, does. Milton opens the poem, for example, with a statement that he is writing it on a more or less empty stomach:

> Mitto tibi sanam non pleno ventre salutem,
> Qua tu distento forte carere potes.

With a stomach anything but full, I send you a prayer for sound health, of which, perhaps, you with your stomach stretched to its uttermost, may be in sore need. (ll. 1–2, CM, 1: 207)

In terms of artistic unity, this establishes a link with the portrait of the abstemious poet developed later. Equally important, given the kind of poet Milton was, is the probability that the lines almost certainly root themselves in autobiographical fact.

The Puritans in general disliked Christmas celebrations and discontinued them when they came into power, laying down as law that December 25 was "to be kept as a fast day, in order that all might call to remembrance their own sins and those of their forefathers in transforming a day sacred to the memory of Christ into an occasion of revelry." Indeed, the thoroughness with which they carried out this legislative fiat would have gladdened the heart of Ebenezer Scrooge himself. "Thus, on a Christmas morning, a little before dinner-time, soldiers were sent round London to search all kitchens and ovens and to carry away any meat they found being cooked."[22]

Milton himself, though fond of quality, was abstemious both in eating and drinking throughout his life. On this point, his early biographers are agreed: Aubrey wrote that he was "temperate" and "rarely dranke between meales"; Toland, that "he was extraordinary temperat in his Diet, which was any thing most in season or the easiest procur'd, and was no Friend to sharp or strong Liquors"; and Jonathan Richardson, that "*Milton* was not Nice, but took what was Set before him. All kinds of Strong Liquors he Hated. Let Those Ask Help from Them who want such Assistance. His Muse needed them not" (*Early Lives,* pp. 6, 194, 207).

Now all the above does not quite establish the factual accuracy of lines 1–2. We do not know Sarah Milton's attitudes toward Christmas dinner, and Milton surely did not feel that altering the details as to his stomach's emptiness was wrong if it enabled him to make his contrast more vivid. Such materials as these, however, do open doors to an aesthetic perception little illuminated by invocations of *personae* or considerations of debate techniques as phenomena isolated from authorial interests and circumstances. That perception is quite simple: learning to talk about oneself within as rigid a set of conventions as those Milton learned is in itself an artistic achievement. Again and again, he uses the conventions, but uses them to say what he genuinely means. In lines 5–8, for example, he writes that his love for Diodati cannot be confined to his chosen meter (the elegiac distich); and while this statement fits nicely into the academic tradition of deprecating one's own efforts, it is also true that after "Elegy 6," Milton did not use the meter again for a long time and then only in epigrams.[23]

Strengthening the connection between the bardic and prophetic poetry and Milton himself are the barely submerged Christian references in the poem's latter portions. As Douglas Bush has justly observed, "In the language of Christian humanism, Jove stands for God," and Milton's reference to the bard's soul and lips alike breathing forth Jove in lines 77–78 as clearly signifies the Christian God as the phrase, "all-judging Jove," in "Lycidas," line 82 (*Var. Comm.*, 2: 666). It is further likely, as Bush suggested, that Milton had in mind in lines 55–58, not only ancient pagan epics, but "also presumably, in spite of the classical language, modern Christian poems, such as Tasso's" (*Var. Comm.*, 1: 121). Indeed, as Anthony Low has observed, the kind of poetry Milton refers to deserves "the title not of epic but divine poetry" ("Unity of *Elegia Sexta*," p. 219). Only the narrowest kind of reading can obscure the connections between the inspired poetry on lofty themes that Milton celebrates in lines 55–78 and his own Nativity Ode, which he refers to in lines 79–90.

A further advantage of acknowledging the autobiographical dimension in the earlier sections of the poem is to see its conclusion, lines 79–88, as far more organically connected with its body than has often been assumed, for there Milton speaks unambiguously of his composition of the Nativity Ode, an autobiographical fact intimately connected to his Christian commitment:

> At tu si quid agam, scitabere (si modo saltem
>   Esse putas tanti noscere siquid agam)
> Paciferum canimus caelesti semine regem,
>   Faustaque sacratis saecula pacta libris,
> Vagitumque Dei, & stabulantem paupere tecto
>   Qui suprema suo cum patre regna colit.
> Stelliparumque polum, modulantesque aethere turmas,
>   Et subito elisos ad sua fana Deos.
> Dona quidem dedimus Christi natalibus illa,
>   Illa sub auroram lux mihi prima tulit.

> If you shall seek to learn what *I* am doing (if only you think it worth your while to seek to know what I am doing), I am hymning the King of Heavenly Seed, Bringer of Peace, and the blessed generations covenanted by the holy books, and the infant cry of God, and the stabling under a poor roof of Him who with his Father cherishes the realms on high, and of the star-begetting skies, of the companies attuning their strains in the high heavens, and of the [heathen] gods of a sudden crushed, at their own fanes. This song I offered as gift on the birthday of Christ; the first light, as the dawn drew near, gave me this song. (CM, 1: 212–15)

Here the autobiographical accuracy of the lines is established both by referral to the Nativity Ode itself and to Milton's lifelong habits of composition. With the exception of the "infant cry of God," all the details he mentions are actually present in the Nativity Ode; and as for his statement, that the first light of dawn gave the song to him, it accords both with the time of day when characteristically he did his best work and with his sense, worked into the ode itself, of the poem as something given to him, not something created by him. The idea of the poem as created outside himself brings us back, full-circle, to literary convention and tradition, but convention and tradition used as media for the transmission of vital facts about Milton himself.

Say Heav'nly Muse

The Muse figure herself, Urania or the "Heav'nly Muse" as Milton calls her in line 15, though pagan in her origin, had been turned into a thoroughly Christian Muse by the time Milton used her. Why and how this should have been are of some relevance in understanding the use that Milton made of her. Of her pagan side, it might be thought that her definition as the Muse of astronomy was the most important fact about her; but although this role of hers undoubtedly led by a process of association to her identification as the Muse of heavenly (that is, Christian) poetry, her nature as inspiratress of art, though shared with her sisters, was a more salient characteristic. If other roles such as patroness of the quietly intellectual or scholarly life were possible for a Muse, there is little of this in her present capacity. I must recapitulate, then, my earlier comments on the Muses as inspirational figures; look at the pagan-Christian conflict as it affected the study and use of mythological materials in general and Urania in particular; then note how Milton related her to the external data of the poem's composition and the psychological experience he underwent in writing it.

In their role as inspiratresses of the arts, the Muses were agents external to the poet that enabled him to achieve a level of excellence in his work inexplicable in terms of his own abilities; and the materials treating of them in this role were so extensive and widely disseminated that Milton's sources cannot with any certainty be established. It is certain, however, that material on the "divine fury" appeared in commonly used grammar-school texts like Erasmus's *Colloquies* and in by no means illustrious reference works of the day.

Very probably, too, Milton during his college years read of it in the *fons et origo* of the tradition, the Platonic dialogues, especially the "Ion" and "Phaedrus." His undergraduate writings contain a number of references to Plato, and no one has ever questioned that Milton read the passage in the "Phaedrus" in which Socrates described the "madness of which the Muses are the source" or the passage in the "Ion" dilating on the power of the Muse:

> She first makes men inspired, and then through these inspired ones others share in the enthusiasm, and a chain is formed, for the epic poets, all the good ones, have their excellence, not from art, but are inspired, possessed, and thus they utter all these admirable poems.

The same holds for all true poets, Socrates maintains, the deity depriving them of their senses

> that we listeners may know that it is not they who utter these precious revelations while their mind is not within them, but that it is the god himself who speaks, and through them becomes articulate to us.[24]

Even had Milton not read such passages, however, he would still have been familiar with these ideas, so widely disseminated were they through his reading. Indeed, as Irene Samuel has argued, his early use of Plato indicates neither specialized knowledge nor interest in that author.[25]

Obviously, lines 15–18 of the Nativity Ode do relate themselves to material like the Platonic passage above:

> Say Heav'nly Muse, shall not thy sacred vein
> Afford a Present to the Infant God?
> Hast thou no verse, no hymn, or solemn strein,
> To welcome him to this his new abode.

The Muse is the figure outside himself actually responsible for the composition of the hymn that follows; and Milton himself, merely her agent.

Milton's designation of his Muse as "Heav'nly," however, introduces another element into his synthesis; he makes his Muse into a Christian one. Once again, this in itself is not a sign of originality on his part. He found ample precedent for his move in work he read outside his academic assignments because many within Milton's society felt keenly the need to reconcile the pagan elements the school system emphasized with the Christian orthodoxy their society upheld.

It is true that some felt material like Muse lore was of absolutely no value to Christians, but the more temperate Augustinian view—that truth is truth wherever it is found—cleared the way for a limited use of such materials. So long as the Christian poet kept his priorities straight, he might find the Muses welcome aid in expressing some perceptions about his own act of composing. After all, the Muses and their like did embody (or so some argued) an admittedly inadequate and fragmented but nonetheless genuine response on the part of pagans to the nature and power of the one God. An expression of this argument that appears in Thomas Godwin's *Roman Antiquities* is especially relevant, for Godwin's book, like Ross's *Mystagogus Poeticus,* was a standard, albeit unpretentious, work that summed up what students were supposed to know. Richard Holdsworth, for example, recommended Godwin for first-year students at Cambridge in the following terms:

> This book is to be read before you come to other Latine authors, as being very usefull in the understanding of them. It acquaints you with the maners & Customs of the Romanes, & so gives life to many Latine phrases, & expressions, which you will meet with in them, so that you shall not much need Commentaries on them: this being as it were a general Comment to them all.[26]

Of some interest, therefore, are Godwin's comments on the matter:

> Though *Satan* had much blinded the hearts of men in old time, yet was not the darknesse of their vnderstanding so great, but that they did easilie perceive, and therefore willinglie acknowledge, that there was some supreame governour, some first mover. . . . But as they were most

certaine, that there was a God, so were they againe very blinde in discerning the true God: and hence hath bin invented such a tedious catalogue of Gods, that as *Varro* averreth, their number hath exceeded thirty thousand, and proved almost numberlesse.[27]

What Godwin pedantically maintained, other more illustrious writers like Richard Hooker, Ralph Cudworth, and Sir Walter Ralegh also affirmed. Hooker's *Laws of Ecclesiastical Polity,* which has often been cited in conjunction with the Nativity Ode, gives the same carefully tempered approval to pagan perception of religious truth, noting how each of their major deities reflected some portion of the true God's nature:

> This workman [God], whose servitor nature is, being in truth but only one, the heathens imagining to be moe, gave him in the sky the name of Jupiter, in the air the name of Juno, in the water the name of Neptune, in the earth the name of Vesta and sometimes of Ceres, the name of Apollo in the sun, in the moon the name of Diana, the name of AEolus and divers others in the winds; and to conclude, even so many guides of nature they dreamed of, as they saw there were kinds of things natural in the world. These they honoured, as having power to work or cease accordingly as men deserved of them. But unto us there is one only Guide of all agents natural, and he both the Creator and the Worker of all in all, alone to be blessed, adored and honoured by all for ever.[28]

Nothing in the above precluded a Christian poet's using these deities, or the Muse, but some four paragraphs later, Hooker adduces material to make that poet charier yet in handling such materials; for some of the pagan deities were nothing less than fallen angels who under many guises had succeeded in getting themselves worshiped as gods:

> Since their fall, their practices have been the clean contrary unto those [good angels] before mentioned. For being dispersed, some in the air, some on the earth, some in the water, some among the minerals, dens, and caves, that are under the earth; they have by all means laboured

to effect a universal rebellion against the laws, and as far as in them lieth utter destruction of the works of God. These wicked spirits the heathens honoured instead of gods, both generally under the name of *dii inferi*, "gods infernal;" and particularly, some in oracles, some in idols, some as household gods, some as nymphs: in a word, no foul and wicked spirit which was not one way or other honoured of men as God, till such time as light appeared in the world and dissolved the works of the Devil. (p. 164)

In short, had Milton's use of mythology been shaped by writers like Godwin or even Hooker, he might well have decided that the risks outweighed the advantages. He concluded differently, of course, incorporating into his work the perception that much pagan lore was polluted at its sources but utilizing those elements he conceived as helpful in expressing his thought. Such was to be his practice from the Nativity Ode to *Paradise Lost,* a practice validated by a long train of writers who offered a more positive approach to such materials than the ones cited above. From Prudentius on, each generation of poets had had to effect its own rapprochement between classical learning and Christian faith. During the Renaissance, the very intensity with which the classics were studied made more noticeable to writers of a religious bent the absence of a Christian poetry comparable to the pagan classics and led to a number of prodigious efforts to create an explicitly Christian poetry in opposition to the pagan; but for Milton, the efforts of writers such as the celebrated Huguenot poet, Guillaume de Salluste, Sieur du Bartas, were merely the latest additions to an ancient and well-defined tradition.

It is difficult to believe that Milton ever read Du Bartas with the kind of reverence he reserved for Homer or Virgil or, more near at hand, Spenser. Still, he did read him, probably in Josuah Sylvester's extremely popular translation, and encountered in Du Bartas's poetic manifesto, *L'Uranie*, possibly for the first time, the classical Muse of astronomy, Urania, transformed into the Muse of Christian poetry.[29] The associative processes—astronomy, heavenly matter, Christian poetry—are obvious enough, and indeed others had used her in a similar manner. It was this poem, however, that made her into the guardian of the movement. In *L'Uranie,* Du Bartas writes that as a young man he had tried to achieve poetic success in all sorts of genres, including dramatic, epideictic, and amatory, but that each of his attempts had been vitiated because in them he did not hold firmly enough to his Christian convictions. From these unfortunate efforts, he was saved by Urania's appearance to him in a vision. Mourning the uses to which poetry had been turned, she promised him literary immortality if only he would limit himself to materials drawn from his Christian faith:

> Abandon then those *Old-wiues-Tales* and *Toyes;*
> Leaue the *Blynd Lad,* who but the blind abuses,
> And only, addle, idle hearts annoyes.
> Hence-forth no more profane the *Sacred Muses.*
> . . . .
> But thou (my Darling) whom before thy birth,
> The *Sacred Nine* that sip th' immortall spring
> Of *Pegasus,* predestin'd to set forth
> Th'Almighties glorie, and his praise to sing:
>
> Although this subiect seeme a barren soile,
> Which finest Wits haue left for fallow fields,
> Yet, doe Thou neuer from this taske recoile:
> For, *what is rarest, greatest, Glorie yields.*[30]

She was, perhaps, overly optimistic; but if posterity was not to yield "greatest Glorie" to Du Bartas's *oeuvre,* it was not for lack of effort on his part nor appreciation on his audience's. All his subsequent poems were attempts to work within the limitations Urania had imposed; and if in his case, the gap between subject and ability was breathtaking, it was a gap that went largely undetected for some time, particularly in England where Josuah Sylvester's translation was more popular than its original ever was in France. Not indeed until near the end of the seventeenth century did Dryden amend his own youthful appreciation of Sylvester's work to curt condemnation of it as "abominable fustian," a view that has pretty well prevailed ever since.[31]

The Mellowing Year

Still, Du Bartas, as rendered by Sylvester, was at the height of a considerable popularity during the very years when Milton was most apt to read him; and some evidence suggests that the older writer influenced him in a number of ways. The psalm paraphrases that he completed at age fifteen contain verbal echoes of Sylvester's translation, and years later Milton was to incorporate one whole line from it into *Paradise Lost*.[32] It is not implausible, then, to argue that Milton's "Heav'nly Muse" owes something to Du Bartas; but as with more illustrious writers like Plato, so here a vast array of conventional materials renders undesirable any talk of a precise source. The words of Urania in his beloved Spenser's *Teares of the Muses*, for example, show that she too is a Christian Muse, urging poets to contemplate "Th' eternall Makers maiestie" and warning that "shame and sorrow and accursed case" await those among them "that scorne the schoole of arts diuine."[33]

To sum up the traditional side of the Miltonic ledger, then, his use of a Muse figure to embody his creative impulses and his Christianization of her to reflect the nature of the work produced by those impulses are conventional and unoriginal. Precisely how, then, did Milton personalize these materials?

He does so by attaching the Christian Muse to the special circumstances of his poem's composition. Du Bartas tells us for example that he was pondering his choice of poetic paths to follow when suddenly Urania appeared to him.

> While, to and fro thus (tossed by *Ambition*)
> Yet un-resolued of my Course, I roue;
> Lo suddainly a sacred Aparition,
> Some Daughter (thinke I) of supernall *Ioue*.
> (p. 529, st. 8)

No specifics are given. Milton, on the other hand, ties his Muse to a very particular time of visitation, early morning before daybreak on the twenty-fifth of December in the year of Our Lord, 1629.

That this is the time of her visitation is made clear by the poem itself, and that this is no poetic fiction is amply documentable. In the poem, Milton asks his Muse whether she has no present for Christ

> Now while the Heav'n by the Suns team untrod,
>   Hath took no print of the approaching light,
> And all the spangled host keep watch in squadrons bright?

In other words before the sun has risen and while the stars are still shining. This accords with his description of the Nativity Ode in "Elegy 6" as "gifts which the first light of dawn brought to me" and with the statement he made a few years later on translating Psalm 114 into Greek verse. Sending a copy of this translation to his friend and former teacher, Alexander Gill, he wrote:

> I send, therefore, what is not exactly mine, but belongs also to the truly divine poet, this ode of whom, only last week, with no deliberate intention certainly, but from I know not what sudden impulse before daybreak, I adapted, almost in bed, to the rule of Greek heroic verse.[34]

It accords too with his description in *Paradise Lost* of his "Celestiall Patroness / Who deigns her nightly visitation unimplor'd."

Milton's own words furthermore are buttressed by supporting statements from others. His eighteenth-century biographer, Jonathan Richardson, for example, wrote "that he frequently Compos'd lying in Bed in a Morning . . . I have been Well inform'd, that when he could not Sleep, but lay Awake whole Nights, he Try'd; not One Verse could he make; at Other times flow'd *Easy his Unpremeditated Verse*, with a certain *Impetus* and *AEstro*, as Himself seem'd to Believe" (*Early Lives*, p. 291).

Entering wholeheartedly into the experience that his Muse offers him, he imagines himself to be in Judea sixteen hundred and twenty-nine years earlier and urges his Muse to anticipate the Wise Men and present her ode to the Lord as His very first gift here on earth. But—and this is important to note—it remains her ode and not his. The mysterious processes whereby the poet is able or unable to write are not his to control, and these processes about which he has read so much now become real to him through the actual experiencing of them.

The Mellowing Year

Looking at Milton's work with the perspective of three hundred years or more, we realize that this datum of his creativity is itself a psychological commonplace. Since Milton, creative persons in many disciplines have written of their own experience in less poetic terms that enable us to see clearly the outlines of the phenomenon. The mathematician, Karl Friedrich Gauss, for example, wrote of years spent in trying unsuccessfully to prove a theorem and then of seemingly miraculous success:

> At last two days ago I succeeded, not by dint of painful effort but so to speak by the grace of God. As a sudden flash of light, the enigma was solved. . . . For my part I am unable to name the nature of the thread which connected what I previously knew with that which made my success possible.[35]

It was not necessarily easy for Milton to accept that inspiration worked in this manner, for it went strongly against the grain of much in his character. He was a hard worker and a careful planner. Years later, he was still to write of "labour and intent studie" as the elements that would enable him to create immortal poetry. And yet the experience of the Nativity Ode was there too and not to be denied. He could not know that only too soon he would experience its reverse, the failure of inspiration as he essayed a companion poem on "The Passion," or that it would take many years more, both of study and of living, before he came finally to terms with the intractable nature of his creativity. He only knew that for the length of time the experience lasted, he was certain that he was one of God's spokesmen: the creative dimension beyond his control *was* heavenly; the poetry of his Muse, as sanctified by God's grace as the lips of the prophet Isaiah had been by the coal of fire drawn from God's earthly altar.

Obviously, the Nativity Ode contains much else besides material about its own composition. It is even true that the elements discussed above constitute a minor portion of the poem as a whole. To the extent that he incorporated himself into the Nativity Ode, however, his treatment owed much to his training. And yet not all. Making the conventions say what he wanted them to, personalizing the impersonal, was his achievement in the parts where he included himself, an achievement that ultimately would impress itself on each line he wrote.

To express his experience of himself as the agent and not the originator of his poetry, he had resorted to the Muses, the stalest of pedantic clichés, and modified them in terms of his outside reading, personal circumstances, and religious faith. Little in these stanzas was brand-new, but they did not read like Du Bartas or Spenser or anyone else. For the first time, he had achieved the turning of his own experiences into great literature, however ordinary the elements he used to express them.

Long Choosing and Beginning Late

LONG before Milton began work on *Paradise Lost,* he had learned how to use the materials of tradition to write an essentially personal poetry. He was long in learning, however, that although he could prepare for the writing of great poetry in all sorts of ways, the act of composition itself was not his to command. Seventeenth-century man that he was, his explanation for this failure was religious rather than psychological: God was the Author of his work, and it was His to give or withhold. So stated, Milton probably accepted this as an abstract principle from early childhood. Before and during the composition of *Paradise Lost,* he learned to accept it existentially through the process of having lived it.

"Legend," as William Riley Parker aptly labeled it, has held that

> Milton's life was preternaturally consistent: that he knew early what he intended to do, set about it simply and directly, never swerved from his determined course, and died with every item on his mental list neatly ticked off as completed.

A fascinating theory, Parker calls this, and he continues:

> since too many persons find Milton almost inhuman to begin with, it has enjoyed a real popularity. But unfortunately, lives are not lived that way, even if a Milton is doing the living. The academic mind—reading into and

between the lines, analyzing and systematizing—is one thing; the artistic mind is another.[1]

Stated as baldly as this, the legend probably no longer has many adherents. In subtler ways, however, it continues to have influence; and in all fairness to academic minds, Milton himself encourages it in many ways, for he was an exceedingly careful planner.

Any refutation of the legend must begin by reviewing the side of his character that led to detailed and systematic planning; trace how his career as a writer, thanks to the vagaries of inspiration, did not at all proceed along the straight, well-marked path he had envisaged; and conclude with explication of how Muse lore works its way into *Paradise Lost*. To it must now be added a new element, the poet's blindness; for Milton's delineation of the inspirational process involves two figures, the blind bard and his Muse.

Janus-like, the passages where these figures appear look backward and forward, backward over the centuries of classical and Christian material condensed into them and forward toward the more radically personal poetry of the Romantics and moderns. Obviously, they are not so "personal" as the effusions of our own contemporaries, but for all that, they are personal. Milton's blindness, his compositional patterns, his choice of subject matter—all these are biographical facts; and all are "in" *Paradise Lost,* transformed certainly by the materials of tradition in which they are bodied forth to their mutual advantage, but there nonetheless.

Thus, Milton's relating his blindness to Thamyris's and Maeonides's gives it a dignity and universality that as a specific biological fact it does not have. On the other hand, our awareness that this comparison roots itself in objective fact vivifies what might easily become stale repetition of worn-out academic matter. The same is true of his Muse, Urania. By relating the facts about his inspiration to the conventional figure of tradition, he elevates them above the merely trivial and temporal. On the other hand, his relating her to the facts of his own life gives her a conviction and a mystery that no writer's Muse since Hesiod had possessed and that no other writer's would again. She illumines his darkness, authors his writing, and encapsulates his poem's major themes.

Most important of all in terms of the interplay between tradition and the individual talent, she need not have been his Muse at all. He might have followed the lead of early Christian poets like Sedulius or Paulinus of Nola and invoked no Muse; or he might well have invoked Calliope or Clio.[2] His choice of Urania underscores how artists, by the materials they use or discard, create their tradition as well as inheriting it. The knowledge that this is so dispenses with the blind reverence for tradition as a reified entity that literary scholars sometimes displayed in the past, but it also encourages a closer look at the materials that constitute tradition.

Labour and Intent Study

In the sketch of Milton as a child, various tributes to his industry and organizational abilities were noted to show how in some respects Milton's character fit in well with the educational practices of his day. It was not merely his willingness to work hard that enabled him to excel in school but also his ability to organize all his work down to the last jot and tittle. Dividing his materials into large though coherent blocks, he tackled each division separately, working his way through each, with no intermission, until he came to a logical stopping point. Specific examples of this he gave in a letter to Diodati, of reading Greek history "as far as to the time when they ceased to be Greeks" and Italian history to the period where "it will be better to read separately what each City did by its own wars."[3]

When he decided to become a poet instead of a priest, he brought to his new goal the same mind-set he had developed as a child and that, in some ways, remained with him throughout his life. This decision, he indicates, the Italian journey crystallized for him:

> In the privat Academies of *Italy*, whither I was favor'd to resort, perceiving that some trifles which I had in memory, compos'd at under twenty or thereabout (for the

manner is that every one must give some proof of his wit and reading there) met with acceptance above what was lookt for, and other things which I had shifted in scarsity of books and conveniences to patch up amongst them, were receiv'd with written Encomiums, which the Italian is not forward to bestow on men of this side the *Alps,* I began thus farre to assent both to them and divers of my friends here at home, and not lesse to an inward prompting which now grew daily upon me, that by labour and intent study (which I take to be my portion in this life) joyn'd with the strong propensity of nature, I might perhaps leave something so written to aftertimes, as they should not willingly let it die.[4]

Naturally, Milton recognizes that labour and intent study are not enough. They must be joined by the strong propensity of nature and may still be thwarted by elements beyond the poet's control like "climat, or the fate of this age." The impression that the passage as a whole leaves, however, is of a man approaching a problem in a clear and orderly way. Having made a general decision, Milton then surveys the generic possibilities open to him; and although this survey is not an infallible guide to what he later did, it is carefully thought out: the epic, divided into diffuse and brief models; the drama; odes and hymns. That great poetry is not written as problems are solved does not come through.

Returning to England, Milton started to work on his newly conceived plans with the same thoroughness he had used to complete the old. To help him give shape to his career as a whole, he had the model of the "Virgilian progression" to contemplate. It was an historical fact that Virgil's works, the *Bucolics, Georgics,* and *Aeneid,* had progressed from a lowly or pastoral style through an intermediate phase to the loftiness of epic; and this fact during the Middle Ages had been elaborated into an all-inclusive wheel, the *rota Vergilii,* that governed everything from the order in which the poet took up his work down to the smallest details he included. Though few, if any, poets managed their writing in complete conformity with this model, its currency in the ones most significant for Milton is obvious in the example of Spenser; for he had begun with pastoral in *The Shepheardes Calender*, progressed to epic in *The Faerie Queene*, and called attention to this in that poem's opening lines:

> Lo I the man, whose Muse whilome did maske,
>   As time her taught, in lowly Shepheards weeds,
>   Am now enforst a far vnfitter taske,
> For trumpets sterne to chaunge mine Oaten reeds,
> And sing of Knights and Ladies gentle deeds.[5]

Looking back over his own work, Milton justifiably felt that he had served his apprenticeship and that the time had come to begin the big project, so he opened a new section, "De Poetica," in his Commonplace Book and began in the Trinity MS to draw up lists of various subjects for plays and dramas and to outline various of those subjects in greater detail, including several drafts of a drama on the story of Adam and Eve.[6]

From large over-arching plans down to the act of composition itself, Milton's orderly habits of thought made themselves felt. When he began even a short poem, he did not pitch right in with the idea that, provided only he scratched around long enough, things would work themselves out. On the contrary, his writing habits closely followed the way he had been taught to write. "The making of Verses," as taught in grammar schools, left little room for spontaneous outpourings, so that Milton early got in the habit of planning his compositions out in his head before he began to set them down. Thus, "At a solemn Musick," the one poem in the canon whose evolution has been preserved on paper, shows clearly that despite the numerous revisions he made, Milton did not begin to write the poem down until he already had a clearly conceived idea of the whole work, knew where he wanted it to go, and how he wanted to say it.[7]

So ingrained in Milton was this habit of ordering and classifying that he applied it retrospectively to the work he completed in the 1640s and 1650s, implying that this truly heterogeneous body of materials had all been written according to a tightly conceived plan, although the outlines of this plan did not become clear to him until after he had completed his anti-prelatical pamphlets. Thus he wrote in the *First Defence* that

> when the bishops, at whom every man aimed his arrow, had at length fallen, and we were now at leisure, as far as they were concerned, I began to turn my thoughts to other subjects; to consider in what way I could contribute to the progress of real and substantial liberty; which is to be sought for not from without, but within, and is to be obtained principally not by fighting, but by the just regulation and by the proper conduct of life. Reflecting, therefore, that there are in all three species of liberty, without which it is scarcely possible to pass any life with comfort, namely, ecclesiastical, domestic or private, and civil; that I had already written on the first species, and saw the magistrate diligently employed about the third, I undertook the domestic, which was the one that remained. But as this also appeared to be three-fold, namely, whether the affair of marriage was rightly managed; whether the education of children was properly conducted; whether, lastly, we were to be allowed freedom of opinion—I explained my sentiments not only on the proper mode of contracting marriage, but also of dissolving it, should that be found necessary. (CM, 8: 131–33)

According to him, then, he wrote his divorce pamphlets in their proper niche, between the anti-prelatical works already finished and the little book on education completed in 1643, and not at all because his failed marriage had in any way engaged his feelings.

This was not the way his contemporaries viewed the matter, even those like Edward Phillips who were certainly on his side. It was Mary Powell's desertion, according to Phillips, that

> so incensed our Author, that he thought it would be dishonourable ever to receive her again, after such a repulse; so that he forthwith prepared to Fortify himself with Arguments for such a Resolution, and accordingly wrote two Treatises, by which he undertook to maintain, That it was against Reason, (and the enjoyment of it not proveable

by Scripture), for any Married Couple disagreeable in Humour and Temper, or having an aversion to each other, to be forc'd to live yok'd together all their Days. (*Early Lives,* p. 65)

The point is not that Phillips was right and Milton wrong, but that such orderly constructs, whether retrospective like the above or prospective like the Virgilian progression, are inadequate maps of reality. As Parker observed, "Lives are not lived that way, even if a Milton is doing the living"; and Milton, Parker notwithstanding, had a generous portion of the academic mind in his makeup. Analyzing and systematizing, he misleads his readers in the above passage, unintentionally, of course, and understandably. Looking back over his work, he may have recalled, as Phillips did not, that he had been interested in the problem of divorce well before his problems with Mary Powell arose, and this perhaps lent credibility in his mind to the plan he now imposed on work completed years earlier.[8] However unintentionally, he still misleads. His problems with Mary Powell did contribute to his decision to write the divorce pamphlets when he did; and his construct gives no sense of the gaps of time between his works or his lack of productivity during certain periods.[9]

In like manner, the Virgilian progression and indeed his whole elaborately organized approach toward the writing of his great work misled himself. The artistic mind simply does not work along neatly ordered lines. One can do everything right, make the most elaborate plans, do all the necessary and proper preparation, and still find that the great work does not materialize or materializes along quite different lines from what one has anticipated. The Muse comes when she is ready, not when the poet is ready, and sometimes she is not at all the one he was expecting.

These data of the creative life Milton had learned to accept by the time he wrote *Paradise Lost;* for despite his well-organized personality, he had had a lifetime of experiencing the fugitive and unpredictable nature of inspiration. How inspiration worked when it worked was discussed apropos of the Nativity Ode. He did his best work in the early morning hours, and this remained his habit throughout his life. This may have been due to his biorhythms, as we would now say, but it also suggests that he did his best when he did not feel under pressure. Confirmation for this exists in the extremely relaxed posture in which he dictated and composed; for in dictating, "he Sat leaning Backward Obliquely in an Easy Chair, with his Leg flung over the Elbow of it," while "he frequently Compos'd lying in Bed in a Morning."[10]

Yet Milton had not been the sort to loll around waiting for the Muse to arrive. Some of his best work, admittedly, arose from conscious and conscientious effort. Early on, however, he had striking confirmation of how hobbling a lack of inspiration could be in completing work that mattered greatly to him. There was, for example, the sequel to his writing the Nativity Ode. Its glorious success might have taught him to rely on the heavenly Muse, but it did not; and the projected companion, "The Passion," was a flop. Perhaps both poems were parts of an intended series commemorating major feast days of the liturgical calendar. Such a series is attractive to the academic mind, though whether that mind was Milton's or James Holly Hanford's is unclear. It was Hanford who years ago suggested such a series as the understood framework for the Nativity Ode, "Upon the Circumcision," and "The Passion," but no external evidence exists to show that Milton himself had such a series in mind.[11] He may have, however, for it would have been in keeping with the well-ordered side of his character. Whether or not he did, his writing of "The Passion" obviously involved a kind of symmetry that looked better in the planning stage than it did when he came to write it.

The interesting feature about "The Passion" is that one can watch the poet striving manfully to keep the work going without inspiration. Like a man on a treadmill, he quite literally goes nowhere. The stanzas tell us what Milton has been writing (the Nativity Ode), what he has been reading (the *Christiad* of the Italian poet Vida), and what he intends to write (an elegy on Christ's death in contrast to Vida's epic treatment of his life). They do not in any sense fulfill that intention. Neither an appeal to "night best Patroness of grief" nor a journey in

Ezekiel's chariot to "where the Towers of *Salem* stood" enables the poet to come to terms with his proposed subject. Extravagant descriptions of his grief suffice to carry him through two more stanzas before he breaks off. Where he might have taken the poem had he continued is anyone's guess. The extant stanzas constitute only a proem to a poem whose envisioned form is impossible to determine.

Perhaps he had similar experience in attempting to write his Arthuriad. Certain lines in "Epitaph for Damon" suggest that he had begun his poem and that he had encountered real problems in writing it:

> Ipse etiam, nam nescio quid mihi grande sonabat
> Fistula, ab undecima jam lux est altera nocte,
> Et tum forte novis admoram labra cicutis,
> Dissiluere tamen rupta compage, nec ultra
> Ferre graves potuere sonos.

I myself too—my pipe was sounding forth some lofty strain, I know not what—another day is come, the day following the eleventh night—I myself, as it chanced, had set my lips to pipes of hemlock, pipes that were new: none the less, bursting their joinings, they leaped asunder, and could brook no longer the weighty strains. (CM, 1: 310–11)

If these lines are to be interpreted literally, they say that he had begun the poem eleven days earlier and that he had found his poetic technique simply not up to the strains that his subject imposed on him.

A few years later, another such experience produced Satan's magnificent apostrophe to the Sun in *Paradise Lost,* IV, 32–41; for Edward Phillips quotes these lines in his biography with the observation that he saw them several years before the poem was begun, Milton having originally intended them for the *very beginning* of a tragedy on the fall (*Early Lives,* pp. 72–73). Since they do not fit into any of Milton's extant plans for tragedies, their composition was almost surely a spur-of-the-moment thing; and thus they represent in an especially acute form Milton's ability to begin a project at a high level of achievement only to find himself very quickly unable to proceed with it.

To correlate, then, with his reading of Plato and others, Milton had a full complement of first-hand experience with the fickleness of the creative process; but the complete integration of his experience and reading was long in coming. Sometime between 1639 and 1641, for example, the story of Cadmon made enough of an impression on him that he jotted it down in his Commonplace Book:

> de Poeta Anglo subito divinitus facto mira, et perplacida historiola narratur apud Bedam. Hist. 1. 4. c. 24
>
> A marvelous and very pleasing anecdote is told in Bede's History about an Englishman who suddenly by act of God became a poet. (CM, 18: 139)

It did not register on him, however, that he, John Milton, might someday stand in need of as striking a display of divine assistance as Cadmon had received. For him, it took a prolonged creative drought to bring home to him how totally dependent on God's grace he was for the completion of his work.

The traditional explanation for this drought has been his occupation with the political and religious struggles of those years. Participation in these struggles meant foregoing his own poetic plans in favor of the prose that was more serviceable to the causes he espoused. This is what he himself said in the *Reason of Church-Government,* where he not only talked at length of his epic plans, but also indicated how handicapped he felt in the polemical warfare that mandated his use of prose:

> Lastly, I should not chuse this manner of writing wherin knowing my self inferior to my self, led by the genial power of nature to another task, I have the use, as I may account it, but of my left hand. (CM, 3: 235)

He then goes on to discuss at length his epic plans, mostly revolving around material drawn from British history, and concludes by covenanting with any knowing reader, that for some yeers yet I may go on trust with him toward the payment of what I am now indebted, as being a work not to be rays'd from the heat of youth, or the vapours of wine, like that which flows at wast from the pen of some vulgar Amorist, or the trencher fury of a riming parasite, nor to be obtain'd by the invocation of Dame Memory and her Siren daughters, but by devout prayer to that eternall Spirit who can enrich with all utterance and knowledge, and sends out his Seraphim with the hallow'd fire of his Altar to touch and purify the lips of whom he pleases: to this must be added industrious and select reading, steddy observation, insight into all seemly and generous arts and affaires, till which in some measure be compast, at mine own peril and cost I refuse not to sustain this expectation from as many as are not loath to hazard so much credulity upon the best pledges that I can give them. (CM, 3: 241)

Polemical context explains much but not everything about this passage. In order to define as sharply as possible the differences separating him from other poets, Milton takes a more austere attitude toward wine and love poetry, Dame Memory and her Siren daughters, than he had earlier or would later. Perhaps this, too, is why he stresses inspiration, however divine in origin, as necessarily to be supplemented by "industrious and select reading, steddy observation," and so on; for he wishes to give his opponents no opportunity to label him an ignorant fanatic. At this point, however, he still had much greater confidence in the efficacy of preparation than he would have later; and this confidence led him seriously to breach the laws of polemic by promising considerably more than he could deliver. Had he covered himself on all fronts, which is polemic's most important law, he would have offered his audience at most a vague promise of great work when the crises of the moment were over. Instead, he asks at most "some few yeers" and thus lays himself open to the charge of always promising much, but delivering little.

Of course, if one accepts that *Samson Agonistes* or portions of *Paradise Lost* and *Paradise Regain'd* were written during these years, no appreciable silence exists to account for; but three decades of controversy on the dating of the major poems have left their traditional chronology more firmly in place than ever.[12] If this chronology is correct, then the evidence that Milton experienced a prolonged period of poetic drought is excellent. Accepting the dating of Edward Phillips for *Paradise Lost's* commencement—"About 2 yeares before the K. came-in"—and taking into account all the above (Darbishire, p. 13), we are left with a sixteen-year hiatus in which Milton composed the following: (1) one substantial (87 lines) Latin poem, "Ad Ioannem Rousium"; (2) twenty lines of Latin verse scattered through the two *Defences;* (3) one four-line Greek epigram; (4) thirty lines of English translation scattered through the prose works; (5) two sets of metrical Psalm paraphrases (774 lines); (6) seventeen sonnets, counting "On the New Forcers" (244 lines); (7) the lines in *Paradise Lost,* IV, 32–41.[13] All these come to a grand total of 1,168 lines, or in the manner of quantification now fashionable, 73 lines a year. Of course, the two sets of Psalm paraphrases, which constitute the bulk of the lines, were all done in April 1648 and August 1653; and if they are excluded, his output is even smaller. Greater exactness is impossible. On the one hand, Phillips speaks of some other verses he was shown along with the ten lines he quotes; on the other, some of the translations could have been written years before he incorporated them into his work. All things considered, his output was meager enough to justify the term, "drought."

The reasons for this drought are not entirely clear. I incline to the view that the failed marriage to Mary Powell was the principal reason for Milton's prolonged silence.[14] At the time of the marriage, however, he had composed no major poem since "Epitaph for Damon," written some years earlier. Probably, then, several factors, including political activity, blindness, ill health, and marital unhappiness, interacted to create the long silence.

Whatever the reasons behind it, a change occurred in the late 1650s. Mysteriously, large blocks of verse did begin to form themselves in Milton's mind, and he could not but note the difference between his current experience of composition and the aborted efforts and long hesitations that had preceded it. The prologues of *Paradise Lost* are his response to this. They, too, have been called constructs; but although they are edited transcripts of the naked truth, they are psychologically more truthful by far than the passage quoted earlier in the *First Defence*.

To their truth, we can add homelier truths of our own. We are more familiar with genuine, as opposed to theoretical, patterns of poetic development so that we are more sympathetic with the problems of the artist struggling into full artistic maturity and more aware of the power that time itself has to bring the process to fruition. We are more aware of the power of the subconscious and can appreciate better than Milton that the poem did progress during years when most of his conscious thoughts were occupied with quite different matters.

In some instances, admittedly, truth shades off into speculation. It may be, for example, that the marriage to Katherine Woodcock was a creatively liberating experience. If, as most continue to think, she is indeed the subject of his twenty-third sonnet, then her appearing to him in a dream and vanishing when he wakes certainly parallels closely his description in *Paradise Lost* of his Muse's nightly visitation; and certainly his resumption of writing poetry follows closely on her death. Unfortunately, we lack sufficient details about their relation to make the above more than an interesting possibility.

At Once Blind, and of the Most Piercing Sight

Such evidential incompleteness does not mute the fact that the truths of the prologues, as Milton perceived them, are confirmed in many ways. None of these is more significant than his blindness; for demonstrably it helped him to recover as an artist so that his portrait of himself as, like Tiresias, blinded to the outer world but rewarded by a compensating inner vision, is substantially true. This initially most crushing of misfortunes proved ultimately to be a great blessing. The sense of loss, the new work habits that had to be learned, the cruel interpretation that so many made of his blindness, all these fed into the depression that was his first response. Coming to terms with them, however, strengthened him. Had he lived in a less theologically dominated era, he might never have bestirred himself to find in his blindness a source of strength. As it was, the accusation that it was God's punishment for his sin in writing against the King prodded him into searching for a more positive way of viewing his misfortune.

These accusations would never have carried the weight they did had they not reflected so widespread an outlook. The doctrine that God used the natural order to punish or reward men as they deserved was the veriest of commonplaces.[15] Thus, the earthquake that touched England in 1580 or the various plague years were viewed as God's direct punishment for England's sins. What then more natural than to interpret Milton's blindness as God's direct response to his impiety in defending regicide? This interpretation was by no means limited to Salmasius, for the *Life Records* provide numbers of parallel statements. Representative of them is Mrs. Anne Sadleir's letter to Roger Williams:

> for meltons book [*Eikonoklastes*] that you desire J should read if J be not mistaken, that Js he that has wrot a book of the lawfulnes of deuorce, and if report sais true he had at that time two or thre wiues liuing. this perhaps were good Doctrine in new England, but it is most abominable in old, England, for his book that he wrot against the late King that you would haue me read, you should haue taken notice of gods judgment upon him who stroke him with blindnes, and as J haue heard he was faine to haue the helpe of one Andrew Maruell or els he could not haue finished that most accurssed Libell, god has began his Judgment vpon him here, his punishment will be hereafter in hell.[16]

As a child of his age, Milton had to come to terms with the fairness of such an interpretation of his misfortune. As a medical fact, he knew that his blindness had been coming on for some years before his involvement with regicide. He also felt that, faced with the choice of preserving the little sight remaining with him and doing his duty as he saw it, he had chosen correctly. Still, he could not let the matter rest there. However much he stressed the long-standing nature of his problems and the heroism of his sacrifice, he was still inclined, as was his age, to believe that God had allowed matters to fall out as they did to some purpose. If that purpose was not punishing him for his sins, then it must be that God had allowed his misfortune to occur so that a greater good might come of it. This belief he was not long in adopting. Having gone over all the above in the *Second Defence,* he ended with the assertion that through his physical blindness he had attained greater inward vision:

> There is a way, and the Apostle is my authority, through weakness to the greatest strength. May I be one of the weakest, provided only in my weakness that immortal and better vigour be put forth with greater effect; provided only in my darkness the light of the divine countenance does but the more brightly shine: for then I shall be at once blind, and of the most piercing sight. Thus, through this infirmity should I be consummated, perfected; thus, through this darkness should I be enrobed in light. And, in truth, we who are blind, are not the last regarded by the providence of God; who, as we are the less able to discern any thing but himself, beholds us with the greater clemency and benignity. Woe be to him who makes a mock of us; woe be to him who injures us; he deserves to be devoted to the public curse. The divine law, the divine favour, has made us not merely secure, but, as it were, sacred, from the injuries of men; nor would seem to have brought this darkness upon us so much by inducing a dimness of the eyes, as by the overshadowing of heavenly wings; and not unfrequently is wont to illumine it again, when produced, by an inward and far surpassing light. (CM, 8: 73)

In the autograph album of Johannes Zollikofer, Milton quoted in Greek 2 Corinthians 12:9, "I am made perfect in weakness," and laboriously signed his name on Sept. 26, 1656 (*Life Records,* 4: 118–19). A few months later, he wrote in the same vein of his blindness:

> Why, in truth, should I not bear gently the deprivation of sight, when I may hope that it is not so much lost as revoked and retracted inwards, for the sharpening rather than the blunting of my mental edge? (CM, 12: 87)

That God could use his blindness to some great purpose is implied in the opening lines of *Paradise Lost,* with their reference to "Siloa's brook" and to another occasion when God had used human blindness to His own advantage:

> And as *Jesus* passed by, he saw a man which was blind from *his* birth.
> And his disciples asked him, saying, Master, who did sin, this man, or his parents, that he was born blind?
> Jesus answered, Neither hath this man sinned, nor his parents: but that the works of God should be made manifest in him.
> I must work the works of him that sent me, while it is day: the night cometh, when no man can work.
> As long as I am in the world, I am the light of the world.
> When he had thus spoken, he spat on the ground, and made clay of the spittle, and he anointed the eyes of the blind man with the clay,
> And said unto him, Go, wash in the pool of Siloam, (which is by interpretation, Sent.) He went his way therefore, and washed, and came seeing.[17]

As Jesus had literally restored this man's vision, so Milton looked for symbolic restoration of his sight, the giving, that is, of insight, and the giving of it to the specific purpose that he might write this poem in a creditable manner. This he spells out most explicitly in his prologue to Book III. After poignantly listing the number of things that he can never see again—

> the sweet approach of Ev'n or Morn,
> Or sight of vernal bloom, or Summers Rose,
> Or flocks, or heards, or human face divine—

he addresses God as Light and asks that in compensation, he be given inner light:

> So much the rather thou Celestial light
> Shine inward, and the mind through all her powers
> Irradiate, there plant eyes, all mist from thence
> Purge and disperse, that I may see and tell
> Of things invisible to mortal sight.

The psychological necessity of Milton's feeling that this was so is obvious enough. Further than that, it has often been argued that a bit of self-dramatization beyond what the facts merit is involved. Another possibility exists, however: that his emphasis on inner vision replacing outer was buttressed by a heightened sense of his own creative powers. The French scholar, Pierre Villey, himself blind, found certain intellectual capacities heightened in his blind state:

> a tendency to reflection and to . . . a certain ponderation. With equal intellectual culture there is, I think, frequently more equilibrium and judgment with the gifted blind man than with the man who can see. That is not surprising, for, the sight is the sense for amusement. The less one is disturbed in this way, the less the inner dream is interrupted by outer events, the more one is concentrated on one's self, the more one takes time to ripen one's reflections, and to weigh the for and against of one's deliberations.[18]

Since it is possible, then, that Milton felt his intellectual ability heightened by his blindness, let me try to correlate his earlier compositional habits with what can be discovered about the compositional habits for *Paradise Lost*. Prior to his blindness Milton's work habits tended to be very orderly. Examination of documents like the Trinity and the Bridgewater MSS leaves no doubt that he worked long and hard on his poems, and yet it is a curious fact that after *Reason of Church-Government*, we hear no more of "labour and intent studie." Indeed, all the comments in *Paradise Lost* stress, rather, the source of poetry as lying outside the poet's conscious control, belonging to

> my Celestiall Patroness, who deignes
> Her nightly visitation unimplor'd,

And dictates to me slumbring, or inspires
Easie my unpremeditated Verse.
(IX, 21-24)

Merely poetic fiction? No. A heightening of the literal truth? Almost surely. External testimony leaves the door ajar to Milton's having revised his work on *Paradise Lost,* and yet his comments do suggest a significant change in emphasis over his earlier attitudes.

The Trinity MS gives evidence that despite his numerous revisions, he had clearly blocked out at least his shorter poems before ever he put pen to paper. John Diekhoff has suggested that in this basic compositional pattern lies the explanation of Milton's successful composing in his blindness:

> It is to his peculiar habit of composition in long "unpremeditated" passages that Milton owed his ability to continue writing even after his blindness: that if he had not been fluent in the production of a first draft, but (like Keats for example) had written line after line by false starts, hesitations, cancellations, working piece by piece toward final form instead of writing long passages to be corrected in detail later, he would not have been able after his blindness to accommodate himself to the method of dictation.[19]

With this, I have no quarrel. Diekhoff surmised, however, that Milton's compositional habits were much the same for *Paradise Lost* as they had been for the short poems in the Trinity MS, that is, that he subjected it to the same kind of laborious line-by-line revision that he gave to poems like "At a solemn Musick."

I suspect that the changes in his compositional habits were rather more drastic; that if, as Villey indicates, concentration is one of the effects of blindness, many of the revisions that Milton formerly made on the page were now made in his head before he began to dictate the passage. None of the contemporary biographers speaks of the composition in such a way as to suggest that much substantive revision was involved. Edward Phillips writes that he had the "perusal of it from the very beginning" in parcels of "Ten, Twenty, or Thirty Verses at a Time, which being Written by whatever hand came next, might possibly want Correction as to the Orthography and Pointing" (*Early Lives*, p. 73). The anonymous biographer tells us only that Milton

> waking early (as is the use of temperate men) had commonly a good Stock of Verses ready against his Amanuensis came; which if it happened to bee later than ordinary, hee would complain, Saying *hee wanted to bee milkd*. (*Early Lives*, p. 33)

His widow told Thomas Birch that Milton "waking in a morning would make her write down sometimes twenty or thirty verses" (*Life Records*, 4: 194–95). Now it is true that Jonathan Richardson in the eighteenth century indicates more of a revisionary process at work than the others:

> I have been also told he would Dictate many, perhaps 40 Lines as it were in a Breath, and then reduce them to half the Number. (*Early Lives*, p. 291)

This would suggest quite a bit more work than merely correcting for orthography and pointing; and to give Richardson his due, a poem as long and artfully done as *Paradise Lost* undoubtedly did involve some revision. Other explanations offer themselves, however, for its impression of careful and painstaking effort: the rigor of his educational experience, years of practice, and years of conscious planning and subconscious mulling over the work before he began. The preponderance of evidence suggests that Milton did not revise extensively once he had dictated his work. Even Richardson emphasizes the flow of verse rather than the revisionary process, suggesting that such post-dictational changes as were made were more in the direction of cutting than of adding or changing. When Milton's Muse was working, she perhaps gave him more than he could use. If this is true, it suggests why he did indeed come to revere the agency that enabled him to compose somewhat differently from the way in which he had previously done.

The qualifying phrase, "somewhat differently," is important. He revised his work less than the Trinity MS suggests had earlier been his norm; and yet easy-flowing, unpremeditated verse was not new to him. This had been his experience in writing the Nativity Ode, Sonnet 7, and in metrically translating Psalm 136 into Greek. Lacking the manuscripts for these poems, we cannot know whether he touched them up a bit once he had them down on paper; but the impression left by his references to their composition is that they came easily and involved a minimum of subsequent work. He had also sometimes begun work on a high level of inspiration only to have inspiration very shortly flag (the tragedy on the fall) and had laboriously tried to write poetry where inspiration was lacking ("The Passion").

What he has to say in the prologues suggests that retrospectively he came to deem these occasions, positive and negative, as more significant than those where he had managed to achieve artistic excellence through intense and prolonged effort. In 1642, he had had only a very few experiences like "The Passion" to suggest that "labour and intent studie" were not enough; in 1658, he had years and years of effort and no result to teach that they were not. Now, again, he found large blocks of material coming unbidden into his consciousness at night or in the early morning hours, the process repeating itself night after night, month after month, year after year. And yet composition was apparently little under his control, unpredictable:

> When he could not Sleep, but lay Awake whole Nights, he Try'd; not One Verse could he make; at Other times flow'd *Easy his Unpremeditated Verse,* with a certain *Impetus* and *AEstro,* as Himself seem'd to Believe. Then, at what Hour soever, he rung for his Daughter to Secure what Came. (*Early Lives,* p. 291)

Edward Phillips suggests that there was a certain regularity to it, that Milton was able to compose successfully only during the colder months of the year:

> There is another very remarkable Passage in the Composure of this Poem, which I have a particular occasion to

remember; for whereas I had the perusal of it from the very beginning; for some years, as I went from time to time, to Visit him . . . having as the Summer came on, not been shewed any for a considerable while, and desiring the reason thereof, was answered, That his Vein never happily flow'd, but from the *Autumnal Equinoctial* to the *Vernal,* and that whatever he attempted was never to his satisfaction, though he courted his fancy never so much; so that in all the years he was about this Poem, he may be said to have spent but half his time therein. (*Early Lives,* p. 73)

If this is true, the very regularity of the timing helped to underscore for Milton how little it lay in his power to control it.

Clearly, then, the lines concerning his Celestiall Patroness's nightly visitation accurately present the facts of his compositional experience. They do not, of course, tell the whole truth, but they tell significant portions of it, heightened by Milton's sure sense of what literary materials will accord with his artistic and personal purposes. It now remains to show how, out of the vast and varied materials of Muse lore available to him he selected and shaped Urania.

Heav'nly Muse

GIVEN HER NATURE and origins, Milton's Urania is a mysterious creature; but her mystery has been compounded by the critics' confusing her with God Himself, also addressed in the prologues. Some years ago, I rather confidently asserted that the presence of two figures in the prologues could be demonstrated syntactically.[1] This was stating the matter with too much force. What I should have said is this: since the prologues' syntax can be construed as involving two entities, the advantages of so construing them should be carefully weighed. If Milton's Muse and God are the same, the problems that arise admit of no satisfactory solution. William B. Hunter's suggestion that the Muse is Jesus Christ involves pronoun ambiguity; Virginia R. Mollenkott's, that Milton's Muse is androgynous, augments his appeal today but is not characteristic of his method. And so on.[2] All of the above objections can be answered, but their cumulative weight suggests the desirability of investigating another approach; for popular opinion notwithstanding, Milton is seldom obscure in the way these interpretations suggest, nor is the argument that two figures are present in the prologues a new one.[3]

Let me begin, then, by looking at the syntax. In the prologue to Book I of *Paradise Lost,* Milton invokes the "Heav'nly Muse" in line 6, but he does not address the Spirit until lines 17–18. Two features suggest that they are not the same: Milton's use of a period at the end of line 16, and the word "chiefly" in line 17. Although there are other places, like line

10, where a period would have been grammatically appropriate, the one at the end of line 16 is in fact the first in the poem.[4] This suggests that Milton here is preparing to introduce a major new element. In addition to the

> Heav'nly Muse, that on the secret top
> Of *Oreb*, or of *Sinai*, didst inspire
> That Shepherd, who first taught the chosen Seed,
> In the Beginning how the Heav'ns and Earth
> Rose out of *Chaos*,

he now—*and chiefly*—invokes that "Spirit, that dost prefer/Before all Temples th' upright heart and pure." Or consider the following lines from Book III:

> Thee I re-visit now with bolder wing,
> Escap't the *Stygian* Pool, though long detain'd
> In that obscure sojourn, while in my flight
> Through utter and through middle darkness borne
> With other notes then to th' *Orphean* Lyre
> I sung of *Chaos* and *Eternal Night*,
> Taught by the heav'nly Muse to venture down
> The dark descent, and up to reascend,
> Though hard and rare.

"Thee" in line 13 has to refer to the "holy Light" that Milton has invoked in the first twelve lines, but if "holy Light" and "the heav'nly Muse" are the same, it is awkward that in addressing the one, he refers to the other in the third person. If the two are the same, it would be more logical for Milton to write "taught by you" in line 19 rather than "by the Heav'nly Muse." The prologues of Book VII and IX and the prologue to *Paradise Regain'd* provide no further evidence for the identity of the two.

To be sure, Book VII of *Paradise Lost* suggests that Milton's Muse is more than just a classical deity:

> Descend from Heav'n *Urania*, by that name
> If rightly thou art call'd whose Voice divine
> Following, above th' *Olympian* Hill I soare,
> Above the flight of *Pegasean* wing.

> The meaning, not the Name I call: for thou
> Nor of the Muses nine, nor on the top
> Of old *Olympus* dwell'st, but Heav'nlie borne,
> Before the Hills appeerd, or Fountain flow'd,
> Thou with Eternal wisdom didst converse,
> Wisdom thy Sister, and with her didst play
> In presence of th' Almightie Father, pleas'd
> With thy Celestial Song.

The lines, however, can be quite adequately explained in terms of Milton's consistent habit of using myth to suggest truth while stressing its inadequacy for such a task. Thus, the architect of Pandaemonium had been famous as a builder even in heaven, though his skill did not save him from ejection with the rest of Satan's crew; and this, Milton tells us, the story of Mulciber reflects, albeit in a distorted way (I, 738–47). The fruits in Paradise, "burnisht with Golden Rind," remind us of "*Hesperian* Fables true, / If true, here only" (IV, 249–50). Disguised as a serpent, Satan sees Eve in a "spot more delicious then those Gardens feign'd / Or of reviv'd *Adonis,* or renownd / *Alcinous,* host of old *Laertes* Son" (IX, 439–41).

If there are two figures in the prologues, we may be sure that Milton had good reasons for including both of them. The appropriateness of God's presence is obvious enough, for Milton had written in *The Art of Logic:* "I suppose that no one doubts that the primal mover of every art is God, the author of all wisdom; in the past this truth has not escaped philosophers" (CM, 11: 11). It was natural then that Milton acknowledge God as the ultimate source of his poetry, and yet to do so was to leave much about his work unexplained. Why, for example, had God's inspiration worked in him to create poetry rather than philosophical discourse; why had it produced the poems we have rather than ones cast in a more traditional epic mold; why did it come to him during the early morning hours; why did it come to him at some times and not at others? An intermediate figure was needed, then, as the agent through whom God's grace, *as it pertained to the poem being written,* could be conveyed. To create such a figure, Milton picked and chose from the materials he had learned as a child, augmented by a lifetime of reading and thinking about the Muses and his own work.

The meaning of Urania becomes clearer if Milton's alternatives are examined. Why, for example, did he choose Urania rather than Calliope or Clio when ample precedent existed for his invoking these sister Muses were he so inclined? To answer this question fully, one must first avoid the trap of anachronism and then read carefully the poetry itself; for Milton's work, though rooting itself in the characteristic usage of his age, transcends that usage. With regard to the first question, the definitions of even the most prestigious of today's reference works must be avoided as reliable guides to Miltonic usage. "Calliope is Muse of the heroic epic, Clio of history . . . Urania of astronomy."[5] If definitions are necessary, a better set for Milton would be the following: Calliope, prime and general representative of poetry; Clio, Muse of history as the Renaissance understood it and consequently of fame, glory, and heroic poetry; Urania, Muse of divine poetry. This, like the preceding set of definitions, turns the living figures of Milton's art into abstractions. Still, when we observe the results of so distinguished a Miltonist as Douglas Bush assigning Calliope's function as "prime and general representative of poetry" to Clio we have to concede the necessity of definitions.

With regard to reading the poetry itself, careful attendance to the actual lines shows that the background as presented has indeed worked its way into the text. Used cautiously, this background illuminates the passages where Milton refers to these Muses and, moreover, the development of his epic thought as well. That epic thought supports those critics who feel that *Paradise Lost* and *Paradise Regain'd* represent a clean break not only with epic tradition in general but also with the epic that he himself originally contemplated writing.

Interpretations of Milton's Clio

Milton alludes to Clio in three of his Latin poems. In "Elegy 4," he pays tribute to his tutor, Thomas Young, in the following lines:

> Primus ego Aonios illo praeeunte recessus
>   Lustrabam, & bifidi sacra vireta jugi,
> Pieriosque hausi latices, Clioque favente,
>   Castalia sparsi laeta ter ora mero.

He led the way for me, when first I traversed Aonia's retreats and the holy greensward of the twice-cleft ridge, [he led the way for me] when I drank Pieria's waters, and, favored by Clio, I thrice sprinkled my happy lips with Castalia's wine.[6]

In "To His Father," he sums up for his father all the wealth that he possesses as insignificant save that which "golden Clio" has given him:

> Sed tamen haec nostros ostendit pagina census,
> Et quod habemus opum charta numeravimus ista,
> Quae mihi sunt nullae, nisi quas dedit aurea Clio
> Quas mihi semoto somni peperere sub antro,
> Et nemoris laureta sacri Parnassides umbrae.

Yet, after all, this page sets forth my rating: all that I have of wealth I have counted out on the sheet that is before you, and yet that wealth is naught save what golden Clio has given me, what slumbers have begotten for me within some grot sequestered, and the laurel-thickets in the holy wood, shady dells on Parnassus.[7]

In "Manso," finally, after praising the Marquis of Manso as a rival of Herodotus himself, Milton salutes him:

> Ergo ego et Clius & magni nomine Phoebi
> Manse pater, jubeo longum salvere per aevum
> Missus Hyperboreo juvenis peregrinus ab axe.

Therefore, in the names of Clio and of mighty Phoebus, I dispatch to you, father Manso, my best wishes for your health through the long, long years, I, a youth from a foreign land, sent from the Hyperborean quarter of the world.[8]

Prime and General Representative of Poetry

The little that has been done on these passages Douglas Bush collects in his variorum commentary on the Latin poems.[9] If he is correct, the allusions to Clio are simply not significant. Of the passage in "To His Father" he writes that "the context shows that Milton is only naming Clio, in a traditional way, as the prime and general representative of poetry; she had acquired that function because, from Hesiod (*Theog.* 77) onward, she commonly came first in lists of the Muses" (p. 241). He makes much the same statement in his notes on "Elegy 4," where he cites his evidence: the passage from Hesiod, G. Linocre's *Musarum Libellum,* and some texts of mnemonic verses once attributed to Virgil (p. 84).

In all fairness, Bush's evidence is solid in that the materials he cites were widespread. The passage in the *Theogony* was the *fons et origo* of information about the Muses; Linocre's *Musarum Libellum* was often reprinted with Natalis Comes's *Mythologiae,* one of the most popular reference works of the Renaissance; the mnemonic verses were undoubtedly the most widely disseminated piece of information about the Muses that the Renaissance possessed.[10] It is true, then, that Clio often, though not invariably, came first in lists of the Muses; true even that she and Calliope vied for honors as greatest of the Muses. When a general representative was desired, however, Calliope was usually chosen. It was she whom Renaissance dictionaries identified as "the goddesse of Poetrie," she whom Platonic tradition identified as the "totality" of her sisters' efforts. In Thomas Cooper's *Bibliotheca Eliotae,* and later his *Thesaurus,* there is, for example, the following entry on her: "One of the nyne Muses, whych excelled all the other in swetenesse of voyce. Of some she is taken for the goddesse of Rhetoryke: of other for the goddesse of poetrie."[11] Cooper's entry "E. K.," whoever he was, more or less followed in glossing Calliope's name for *The Shepheardes Calender:* "one of the nine Muses: to whome they assigne the honor of all Poetical Inuention, and the firste glorye of the Heroicall verse. other say, that shee is the Goddesse of Rhetorick: but by Virgile it is manifeste, that they mystake the thyng."[12] He then quotes from the mnemonic verses, which assign rhetoric to Polymnia.

The widespread tradition that linked the Muses with the spheres and their music also reinforced Calliope's claim as most representative Muse. In Book X of the *Republic*, Plato had stated that each of the heavenly spheres had an attendant Siren: "borne around in its revolution and uttering one sound, one note, and from all the eight there was the concord of a single harmony."[13] These Sirens antiquity sometimes identified with the Muses; but since there were nine Muses (at least according to the dominant tradition) and there were only eight spheres, what was to be done with the ninth Muse? By the end of antiquity she was generally conceived as representing the harmony that the other eight produced and was identified as Calliope. In the late fourth or early fifth century, Macrobius made the whole matter quite clear in his *Commentary on the Dream of Scipio:*

> Moreover, cosmogonists have chosen to consider the nine Muses as the tuneful song of the eight spheres and the one predominant harmony that comes from all of them. In the *Theogony,* Hesiod . . . to show that the ninth was the greatest, resulting from the harmony of all sounds together . . . added: "Calliope, too, who is preeminent among all." The very name shows that the ninth muse was noted for the sweetness of her voice, for Calliope means "best voice." In order to indicate more plainly that her song was the one coming from all the others, he applied to her a word suggesting totality in calling her "preeminent among all."[14]

The tradition that Macrobius has clarified for us persisted during the Renaissance. Comes's *Mythologiae* reproduced the same information (bk. VII, chap. xv), while Macrobius himself was widely read. Erasmus recommended him for study in "De Ratione Studii."[15] "E. K." alluded to him in the general argument of *The Shepheardes Calendar* and may indeed, as W. L. Renwick has written, have "had his Macrobius by him as he wrote."[16] George Sandys listed him among the writers to whom he was indebted in preparing the commentaries that accompanied his translation of Ovid and referred to him specifically in discussing the Muses and their spheres, Calliope being "the melody which results from the rest."[17] Singly and together these works reinforced each other. In his *New Discovery of the Old Art of Teaching Schoole,* Charles Hoole listed Sandys's *Ovid* along with Comes and other works as appropriate for inclusion in a school library.[18] I am discussing, then, a widespread tradition, not an isolated author or two.

That Milton was directly familiar with the Platonic passage is clear from the second prolusion (CM, 12: 150–51). By his day, however, there were generally considered to be nine spheres instead of eight; and this is the number he associates with the Sirens or Muses in "Arcades," lines 62–64. Still, when the popularity of writers like Comes and Sandys is considered, it would not be surprising if Milton used Calliope as the most representative of the Muses. Although he does not refer to her by name in any of his finished work, a preliminary version of *Lycidas* in the Trinity MS reads:

> what could the golden hayrd Calliope
> for her inchaunting son
> when shee beheld (the gods farre sighted bee)
> his goarie scalpe rowle downe the Thracian lee.

It is instructive to compare this with his final revision:

> What could the Muse her self that *Orpheus* bore,
> The Muse her self for her inchanting son
> Whom Universal nature did lament,
> When by the rout that made the hideous roar,
> His goary visage down the stream was sent,
> Down the swift *Hebrus* to the Lesbian shore.
> (ll. 58–63)

His substitution of the general for the specific suggests a view of Calliope as representative, a view that her role as mother of Orpheus, the archetypal poet, sustains. The sense of the passage, that is, dictates that we identify "the Muse" as the one most nearly capable of patronizing all poetry. With an important caveat, to be examined later, this identification explains

Milton's same use of her, again unnamed, in *Paradise Lost:* "nor could the Muse defend / Her Son" (VII, 37–38). Which Muse? Surely the context suggests that the most representative one is intended.

Guardian of Lustration

John T. Shawcross first advanced this interpretation a number of years ago and has repeated it in both his editions of Milton's poetry.[19] From the *Theogony* he noted a reference to the Muses as "bestowers of talents"; from Plutarch's *De Pythiae Oraculis*, Simonides's labeling of Clio as "holy guardian of lustration" at the Muses' shrine at the mountain spring.[20] As guardian of the purification that metaphorically bestowed the Muses' gifts, "Clio in her later role as muse of history became the guardian of man's individual history, that is, the guardian of what a man was given and what he was to become because of those talents." Clio's gifts, then, enabled Milton to write poetry at an early age ("Elegy 4") and indeed constituted the sum total of his "abilities and capabilities" ("To His Father").

In his annotations to the minor poems, John Carey referred both to Simonides's fragment and to Shawcross's interpretation, implying a difference of opinion. Shawcross, writes Carey, "thinks Clio . . . 'the personification of man's individual history', but cites no classical precedent. It seems more likely that she is named as guardian of lustration."[21]

Bush rejects this as "abstruse," as in truncated form it is (*Var. Com.*, pp. 85, 242). But because Renaissance historiography emphasized far more than modern the deeds of the individual, the view does not seem nearly so abstruse. In order to see its aptness we need only recall such definitions of history as Jacques Amyot's: "an orderly register of notable things said, done, or happened in time past, to mainteyne the continuall remembrance of them, and to serve for the instruction of them to come."[22] Milton's own statement of purpose in his *History of Britain* parallels these words closely: "to relate well and orderly things worth the noting, so as may best instruct and benefit them that read" (CM, 10: 3). So long as we are careful to remember that Clio was not the guardian of the history of Everyman, but of the few who did heroic deeds or set them down, this interpretation brings us closer to the heart of the matter than Bush's.

Muse of History

A majority of the critics, however, have identified Milton's Clio as the Muse of history, though their explanations as to why the Muse of history should appear in the passages quoted have not on the whole been very satisfactory. Of "To His Father," David Masson writes that Milton refers to Clio "inasmuch as what he is to say about his Father is strictly true,"[23] a statement that Walter MacKellar endorsed in his edition of the Latin poems.[24] A. S. P. Woodhouse states rather tentatively that "if the allusion is to historical reading, it reminds us of the enthusiasm for history expressed in Prolusion 7."[25] Milton's allusion, William Riley Parker maintains, refers "to the study of history ('Clio', 14) which Cambridge did not provide but is now possible" (*Milton*, p. 789). Merritt Y. Hughes states: "If Milton meant anything in particular by referring to Clio, the Muse of history, it was the glory that he hoped to win for himself and his country by writing poetry based on the heroic past of England."[26]

I believe that Milton did indeed mean something in particular by referring to Clio and that the critics' failure properly to identify that something is their failure to come to terms with the Renaissance concept of history or to relate that concept to its most notable mythological embodiment. Certainly when Amyot's or Milton's words are recalled, it is not surprising to discover that Clio was ubiquitously associated with fame and glory; yet of the statements in the preceding paragraph, only Hughes's even obliquely touches upon this association, and ironically he dropped it from his later edition of Milton's poetry.[27] Once this association is understood, the key to Milton's use of Clio is possessed.

CLIO, MUSE OF HISTORY, FAME, AND GLORY

From his youth Milton was exposed to a large body of materials that specifically asserted Clio's connection with fame and glory. The reference works known to have been in the library at St. Paul's are unanimous on the point. The general entry on the Muses in Friar Ambrosius Calepinus's *Dictionarium Octo Linguarum* stated: "Primam enim a bonitate vocis dixere Calliopen, Secundam Clio, a gloria & celebritate rerum gestarum, quas canit: quae eadem Historica dicitur."[28] ("The first one, then, they call Calliope from the goodness of her voice. The second one, Clio, from the glory and fame of the warlike exploits of which she sings, which likewise are called history.") He thus draws a connection, as practically all Renaissance mythographers did, between Clio and the Greek word *kleos*, which means fame or glory. In his separate entry for her, Calepinus made another connection explicit: "κλίω, Vuna [*sic*] Musarum ex novem, apud Hesiodum in Theog. ἀπὸ τοῦ κλέους: id est, a gloria, quod poetis gloria ex carmine nascatur" ("*klio*, one of the nine Muses, in Hesiod's *Theogony apo tou kleous:* that is, glory because glory is born to poets from their songs"). Carolus Stephanus, in the general entry on the Muses in his *Dictionarium Historicum ac Poeticum,* used exactly the same words that Friar Calepinus had in his, while in his entry on Clio he repeated Calepinus and added: "Alii ἀπὸ τοῦ κλείειν, hoc est, a celebrando dictam putant, propterea quod historiae inuentrix esse putetur: cuius proprium est virorum fortium laudes celebrare, eorumque gesta ad posteritatem transmittere."[29] ("Others claim that the word comes from *apo tou kleieiu,* that is, from *celebrando,* especially because she is said to be the inventress of history, of whom it is appropriate to celebrate the praises of brave men and transmit their deeds to posterity.") In his entry for Clio, Robertus Stephanus defined similarly: "Vna ex musis, a gloria & celebritate rerum gestarum quas canit: nomen habet a verbo Graeco κλείω, quod est laudo. Vel a nomine Graeco, κλέος, quod est gloria, fama."[30] ("One of the Muses, from the glory and celebration of the deeds she sings: she has her name from the Greek verb, *kleio*, that is, praise, or from the Greek noun, *Kleos,* that is, glory, fame.")

Other well-known works of the period tell the same story. In Cesare Ripa's *Iconologia,* for example, we read: "Questa Musa e detta Clio, dalla voce Greca κλέα, che significa lodare, o dall'altra κλέως, significante gloria, & celebratione delle cose, che ella canta, overo per la gloria, che hanno li Poeti presso gli uomini dotti, come dice Cornuto, come anco per la gloria, che ricevono gl'huomini, che sono celebrate da Poeti."[31] ("This Muse is called Clio, from the Greek word *klea,* which means to praise, or from the other *kleos,* signifying glory and the celebration of the things that she sings, or on account of the glory that the poets have among learned men, as Cornutus says, as also on account of the glory that men receive who are celebrated by the poets.")

Finally, in the tradition that associated the Muses with the spheres, Clio's was Mars. The reason Sandys succinctly expressed: "*Clio* of Mars, for the thirst of glory" (p. 248).

As background material these quotations could be greatly augmented, but they suffice to illuminate Milton's thought on Clio, history, and epic writing. Almost unanimously they assert Clio's power not only to bestow fame and glory upon those whose deeds deserve them but also (for Milton most significantly) upon those who record the deeds. No doubt can exist that Milton long believed this, as his own writings show: "Worthy deeds are not often destitute of worthy relaters: as by a certain Fate great Acts and great Eloquence have most commonly gon hand in hand, equalling and honouring each other in the same Ages";[32] or "Indeed from my youth upward I had been fired with a zeal which kept urging me, if not to do great deeds myself, at least to celebrate them."[33] His celebration would be for the most part in poetry, and that branch of poetry that celebrated the loftiest actions was of course the epic, a genre that belonged at least as much to Calliope as to Clio. At this point, however, it should be clear that the recording of historical material in epic poetry had about it nothing of the eccentric and that associations with Clio were not lacking if the poet wished to develop them.

When Milton wrote "Elegy 4," he almost certainly had not

decided to become an epic poet. The Renaissance educational system stressed "good fame" as one of its rewards, and the passage in "Elegy 4" tells us that in some genuine sense Milton felt that his education began with Thomas Young. Through Young's guidance he first surveyed the Aonian retreats. ("Primus ego Aonios illo praeeunte recessus / Lustrabam. . . .") The allusion to Clio strengthens the probability that Milton refers here to the commencement of his education. A passage from the sixth-century writer Fulgentius the Mythographer makes clear why and provides yet another link to fame. Identifying the Muses as the stages of learning and knowledge, Fulgentius designated Clio as the first step: "First is Clio, standing for the first conception of learning, for *cleos* is the Greek for fame. . . . Since no one seeks knowledge except that by which he may advance the honor of his reputation, Clio is named first, that is the conception of the search for knowledge."[34] Fulgentius's ideas were picked up by Boccaccio in his *De Genealogiae Deorum gentilium* (bk. XI, chap. ii), whence they passed into the general store-house of Renaissance mythography. The passage above was reprinted for example in Linocre's *Musarum Libellus,* Hyginus's *Fabularum Liber,*[35] and Gyraldus's *De Musis Syntagma.*[36]

There is then an aptness in Milton's allusion to Clio. It was Young who introduced Milton to the glories of learning, perhaps as Shawcross suggests to the writing of poetry.[37] Perhaps Young did not literally start Milton in "making of Verses," but rather showed him how such exercises could become more than merely schoolboy drudgery. The specifics are lacking, but heightened awareness of background clarifies the passage's significance: in a sense important to him, Milton felt that his education began with Young. It was to be some years before he acquired the confidence that he "might perhaps leave something so written to aftertimes, as they should not willingly let it die,"[38] but the desire to fit himself for such writing was already his, as he later indicated. It was a desire attached to concepts of history and serious poetry of which he would become increasingly aware with the passage of years.

At some point awareness turned to the commitment reflected in "To His Father," where Milton next alludes to Clio.

He begins with an admission that his Muse's work so far has not been very significant:

> I would fain have the Pierian springs divert, at this instant, their water courses, through my breast; I would fain have the stream loosed from the twin peaks and roll, in all its fulness, o'er my lips, to the end that, forgetting all humble strains, my Muse may rise on daring pinions to discharge her loving service to my father, a father worthy of all reverence.

The posture that Milton assumes in these lines was *de rigueur* for the poet who felt he had served his apprenticeship and was ready to embark upon his major work. Following now consciously in the footsteps of Spenser and (at a greater distance) Virgil, Milton recognizes "To His Father" as a digression, but a necessary one. His song to his father is a poor attempt to repay a debt that cannot in any case be repaid. Nevertheless, he attempts to do so out of what he has, using the paper he writes on to sum up whatever abilities he has, which are insignificant except for those bestowed by "golden Clio."

The paper itself then tells us what Clio has given, her gifts in turn defining her own nature more clearly. Since it contains a poem, her gifts must include poetry. The conventional attitude he began with, he maintains: his Muse's trifling songs are best forgotten; "To His Father" is a poor attempt, mere "sport and frolic" (line 115). On the other hand, lines 17–66 constitute a long statement on "song divine, creation of the bard." The concept of poetry that he invokes—religious, prophetic, mysteriously powerful—is not new to him. He had touched on it in "At a Vacation Exercise," "Elegy 6," the Nativity Ode, and "Il Penseroso," for example, but the concreteness with which he attaches himself to it is new. This Clio's other gifts explain, especially the magnificent education that Thomas Young had instituted and that Milton after a brief address to his father (lines 56–66) goes on to describe at length (lines 67–91). As a result of this education, however inadequate the "song of my youth," he is now convinced that he can do great things:

Therefore, since I am already a part, albeit the lowliest, of the learned [poetic] throng, I shall sit amid the victors' crowns of ivy and of laurel.

"Manso," "Epitaph for Damon," and the listings in the Trinity MS indicate that the great things were to include an epic, and it is easy to establish what its general nature, if not its precise subject, was to be. In his *Poetics,* Scaliger had written that "epic poetry . . . describes the descent, life, and deeds of heroes."[39] Even the Christian version of this that Milton gave in the *Reason of Church Government* had ample precedent, for he aligned himself with Tasso and others, especially Spenser, in speculating on "what K. or Knight before the conquest might be chosen in whom to lay the pattern of a Christian *Heroe*" (CM 3: 237).

Epic theory and practice, in short, marked out clearly the path the aspiring poet was to follow. I stated that the epic belonged at least as much to Calliope as to Clio, though connections with Clio were not lacking if the poet wished to develop them. One might state the matter more strongly: the Miltonic background mandated a careful consideration of Clio as epic Muse. The copious citations that O. B. Hardison, Jr. has collected from Renaissance and earlier writers on the relation of epic, history, and fame, though not addressed specifically to the choice of a Muse, are relevant.[40] More to the point is Spenser's choice of Clio as Muse of *The Faerie Queene.* Spenserians have debated the matter at length, but the evidence—then current definitions of history, the etymologies of her name, its accord with his designation of Elizabeth as Gloriana and her capital as Cleopolis—all indicate Clio. Given Spenser's reputation for idiosyncrasy, finally, it is noteworthy that numerous quotations can be culled from seventeenth-century writers to suggest that his choice of a Muse at least was not regarded as unusual. Dr. Adam Littleton in his *Latine dictionary,* for example, gave the following definition for Clio: "One of the nine *Muses,* and she the first *Hes.* whence *Ovid* calls the rest her Sisters. She was the Mistress of History, and the Patroness of Heroick Poets."[41]

"Manso," the last poem in which Milton alludes to Clio, suggests that the epic projected in the late 1630s and early 1640s would have conformed to Scaliger's dictum and to Spenser's example, and that an important element was to be the reciprocal glory with which Clio was associated.

This glory accords nicely with the references to the poem's recipient, for the Marquis of Manso both derived glory from his association with Tasso and Marino and also, through his biographies of them, helped to preserve their glory. These biographies make him in Milton's estimation a rival to Herodotus himself. Not surprisingly, then, Milton salutes him "in the names of Clio and mighty Phoebus." The following lines, however, contain allusions to Clio not generally recognized:

> Nec tu longinquam bonus aspernabere musam,
> Quae nuper gelida vix enutrita sub Arcto
> Imprudens Italas ausa est volitare per urbes.
> Nos etiam in nostro modulantes flumine cygnos
> Credimus obscuras noctis sensisse per umbras,
> Qua Thamesis late puris argenteus urnis
> Oceani glaucos perfundit gurgite crines.

Since you are so gracious, you will not spurn a Muse that comes from afar, a Muse that, though nurtured but hardly 'neath the cold Bear, unthinkingly dared, recently, a flight through the cities of Italy. I too, I am persuaded, have heard through the dark shadows of the night the swans as they attuned their strains in my own river, where the silvery Thames, bright-urned, wide-spreading stream, drenches his grey tresses with the swirling waters of ocean. (27–33)

The Muse that comes from afar here is Milton himself, its denotation of "poet" being one that he used several times, for example, in "Elegy 1," line 69, and "Lycidas," line 19. It is not clear, however, why he has heard swans singing. The proverbial nature of the Thames's swans (at least in England) might be thought adequate explanation except for the Italian nationality of the poem's intended recipient. That considered, an allusion to Clio is more adequate, for it is certain that Clio and swans were frequently associated in Italian representations of

Figure 1. From a series of early sixteenth-century frescoes, Umbrian School. Clio, Muse of history, in a characteristic pose with swans and pseudo-Virgilian verse in background. (Reproduced by courtesy of Martinus Nijhoff and the Capitoline Gallery)

Figure 2. Ferrarese engraving. Clio with swan. (Reproduced courtesy of Martinus Nijhoff and the Trustees of the British Museum)

the Muses (figures 1 and 2).[42] Milton has heard swans singing because they are associated with Clio, in whose name he has greeted the marquis; he has heard them singing in England because his homeland is not lacking in a heroic tradition in poetry:

> (Gens Druides antiqua sacris operata deorum
> Heroum laudes imitandaque gesta canebant),

(The Druids, a time-honored race, busied with the holy rites of the gods, were wont to sing the praises of the heroes, and their achievements worthy of imitation.) (42–43)

When in concluding Milton writes of the fame he hopes to achieve through a great epic about "the kings of my native land, and Arthur . . . or . . . the high-hearted heroes bound together as comrades at that peerless table," the implication is that his work is part of an established tradition, the most fitting representative of which is the Muse already invoked in a great poem about Arthur, the Muse of history, fame, and glory—Clio.

CLIO AND URANIA

That epic, however, he never completed; and interestingly enough after the early 1640s, Clio disappears from his poetry, never to return. When he came to compose *Paradise Lost*, it was a very different epic he wrote and a very different Muse, Urania, whom he invoked. Personal and public experience had made it impossible for him to reconcile Clio's values with those of Christianity as he increasingly understood them. This was indeed a major development in his thought, and the figures of Clio and Urania, coupled as they often were, may well have played a key role in clarifying that change to Milton and the expression it must now take.

The frontispiece of the 1645 edition of Milton's poems (figure 3) contains around the so-called Marshall portrait four Muses: Melpomene, Erato, Urania, and Clio.[43] We do not know whether these iconographic embellishments were added

Figure 3. Frontispiece of the 1645 edition of Milton's poems, with four Muses surrounding the poet's portrait. Significantly, Urania gazes toward the heavens; Clio, toward the earth. (Courtesy of the Lewis Collection, Texas Christian University Library)

at Milton's suggestion or whether Marshall simply pulled them out of a storehouse of appropriate figures. It is certain, however, that the pairing of Urania and Clio at the bottom of the frontispiece was not Marshall's invention. Long before, the Italian musicologist Gafurius had placed the two Muses at opposite ends of the celestial octave depicted in the frontispiece of his own *Practica Musicae*, the highest note belonging to Urania, "who was frequently represented in an averted posture gazing at the stars, while the first and lowest note (Clio) was compared by Gafurius to 'the sigh of Proserpina', breaking (as he said) the silence of the earth"[44] (see figure 4). In the sixteenth century, an engraving of Marcantonio Raimondi after Raphael represents the Muses of history and astronomy (figure 5). "Touched by the celestial music of the spheres, Urania has closed her book and appears to be seized with an ecstatic rapture, whereas Clio, bound to the earth, records the deeds to be remembered."[45] There is nothing novel, then, in Marshall's representation of Urania with her spheres, eyes turned upward toward the heavens, coupled with Clio writing in her book, eyes cast toward the ground.

As Milton looked at these figures, we can assume that he was familiar with a portion at least of the material that constituted their iconographic background, for some of it was quite common. Literature as well as iconography reflected it. Consider, for example, Urania's lines in Spenser's *Teares of the Muses*. Let the ordinary run of poets despise her if they will, she says,

> How euer yet they mee despise and spight,
> I feede on sweet contentment of my thought,
> And please my selfe with mine owne selfe-delight,
> In contemplation of things heauenlie wrought
> So, loathing earth, I looke vp to the sky,
> And being driuen hence, I thether fly.
>
> (ll. 523–28)

Urania's essence, whether portrayed in an averted posture or with her eyes turned toward the heavens, was renunciation, a frank indifference to the things of this world.

Clio's values were those habitually labeled classic and pagan; Urania's, Christian. In his earlier years, Milton may not have

Figure 4. Figures analogous to Clio and Urania on the title page of Hyginus's *Astronomi de Mundi et Sphere,* Venice, 1502. (Courtesy of the Department of Rare Books and Special Collections, The University of Michigan Library)

Figure 5. Engraving by Marcantonio Raimondi after Raphael. "Touched by the celestial music of the spheres, Urania has closed her book and appears to be seized with an ecstatic rapture, whereas Clio, bound to the earth, records the deeds to be remembered." (From a private collection)

felt any great tension between the two, for the Renaissance humanists had effected a remarkable, if unstable, synthesis of the classic and Christian. When, therefore, he confessed to Diodati his longing for "an immortality of fame," he probably felt his sentiment consonant with his duties as a Christian, supportable if necessary by referral to writers like Castiglione and Sir Thomas Elyot, who had urged the value of glory and honor, and whose Christianity was not in question.[46]

So too with his attraction to military topics: it was consistent not only with epic tradition in general but with the Christian writers like Tasso and Spenser whom he most admired. In *The Faerie Queene,* Red Cross Knight, with Contemplation as his guide, had been confirmed in his impression that Cleopolis was nothing in comparison with the new Hierusalem; but although Contemplation warned him of the dangers inherent in earthly conquest, he nevertheless stated that Cleopolis was

>   for earthly frame,
> The fairest peece, that eye beholden can:
> And well beseemes all knights of noble name,
> That couet in th' immortall booke of fame
> To be eternized, that same to haunt,
> And doen their seruice to that soueraigne Dame,
> That glorie does to them for guerdon graunt:
> For she is heauenly borne, and heauen may iustly vaunt.
>   (I, x, 59)

The humanists, however, never obliterated the more austere view that St. Augustine had expressed, that "contempt of glory is a great vertue: because God beholdeth it, and not the iudgement of man."[47] Horace's boast that he had "finished a monument more lasting than bronze and loftier than the Pyramids' royal pile" acquired in writers like Dante a poignancy from the Christian's knowledge that earthly glory was the sum total of the pagan poet's reward.[48] In Canto xxiv of the *Inferno,* Virgil warns Dante that

>   sitting on down,
>   or under coverlet, men come not into fame;

> without which whoso consumes his life, leaves
> such vestige of himself on earth, as smoke
> in air or foam in water.⁴⁹

But as we all know, Virgil, however noble, is finally and irrevocably damned along with many others who, judged by classical standards, are worthy only of praise. The praise in fact they receive, but not salvation; and indeed of all the souls that Dante meets in the other world, only those in hell seem concerned about the memory, good or bad, that they have left behind. In Canto xi of the *Purgatorio,* Oderisi comments at length on the vanity of artistic pride that was his sin:

> O empty glory of human powers! How short
> the time its green endures upon the top, if it
> be not overtaken by rude ages!
>
> Cimabue thought to hold the field in painting,
> and now Giotto hath the cry, so that the fame
> of the other is obscured.
>
> Even so one Guido hath taken from the other
> the glory of our tongue; and perchance one
> is born who shall chase both from the nest.
>
> Earthly fame is naught but a breath of wind,
> which now cometh hence and now thence,
> and changes name because it changes direction.
>   (ll. 91–102)⁵⁰

No need exists to fit all of Milton's statements on fame and glory to a Procrustean bed, but one can observe that the general direction of his thought was toward the Augustinian view. The most significant proof of this is the epics that he finally wrote. Notably unlike their predecessors, they are, as John M. Steadman has written, "Milton's condemnation of virtually the entire epic tradition, the final humiliation of the conventional heroic ideal."⁵¹ If his final thoughts on the value of fame and glory are expressed with an unprecedented bluntness, a part of the explanation lies perhaps in the figures of Clio and Urania, who for him most notably summed up desire for and contempt of fame.

URANIA

Of Urania, I have already said much, noting her use in writers like Du Bartas and in earlier Miltonic work like the Nativity Ode. In terms of his sense that he was merely the conduit and not the originator of his work, his inclusion of a Muse is understandable; in terms of the specifically Christian subject matter of *Paradise Lost,* his invocation of Urania is predictable; in terms of the poem we have, finally, his choice was absolutely right.

He was right, to begin with, in that *Paradise Lost* is a poem, a work, that is, whose author reveals his meaning through art rather than theological or philosophical discourse. This explains the mysterious lines about Urania's playing with her sister "Wisdom" (VII, 7–12). To William B. Hunter and others, their phrasing has suggested Proverbs as the passage's ultimate source:

> The LORD possessed me in the beginning of his way, before his works of old.
> I was set up from everlasting, from the beginning, or ever the earth was.
> When *there were* no depths, I was brought forth; when *there were* no fountains abounding with water.
> Before the mountains were settled, before the hills was I brought forth. (8:22–25)

In *Christian Doctrine* Milton wrote "that it is not the Son of God who is there introduced [as had sometimes been maintained], but a poetical personification of wisdom" (CM, 15: 13). In *Paradise Lost* Milton has turned the one figure of Proverbs into two. William B. Hunter has plausibly explained his doing so as Milton's way of representing two of Christ's manifestations, Divine Beauty and Divine Wisdom, or as the result of Milton's "using 'sister' as a metaphor for self-identity: the Greek 'Heavenly Beauty' is the same being as the Hebrew 'Wisdom' in that they had been used to express a second deity in two different cultures."[52] Urania might better be identified, however, as a "poetical personification" of Divine Art. As such, she is, of course, closely related to Wisdom. Indeed, looking again at a sentence from *The Art of Logic* quoted earlier, we can note that it easily translates into a metaphor, with God as the father, Art and Wisdom as sisters: "the primal mover of every art is God, the author of all wisdom." Furthermore, it is most natural that the figure who now inspires Milton in his artistic efforts should have been present with God and Wisdom from the beginning, for the image of God as Artist was very old and had been popular during both antiquity and the Middle Ages. To go back no further than the orthodox and unoriginal Du Bartas, he had filled his works with comparisons of God and human artists, as in "The seaventh Day of the first Weeke," for example, where he compared God's feelings in finishing his creation with those of a "cunning Painter."[53] Urania, then, is a fit figure to inspire Milton as he reveals God's wisdom in the form of art, specifically religious poetry.

The prologue to Book I of *Paradise Lost* provides further evidence of the close relation between wisdom and religious poetry that Milton felt, and outlines the part of his purpose that he will more definitely define in Book IX, the writing of a Christian epic that will have nothing in common with its predecessors in the epic genre:

> Of Mans First Disobedience, and the Fruit
> Of that Forbidden Tree, whose mortal tast
> Brought Death into the World, and all our woe,
> With loss of *Eden*, till one greater Man
> Restore us, and regain the blissful Seat,
> Sing Heav'nly Muse, that on the secret top
> Of *Oreb*, or of *Sinai*, didst inspire
> That Shepherd, who first taught the chosen Seed,
> In the Beginning how the Heav'ns and Earth
> Rose out of *Chaos:* Or if *Sion* Hill
> Delight thee more, and *Siloa's* Brook that flow'd
> Fast by the Oracle of God; I thence
> Invoke thy aid to my adventrous Song,
> That with no middle flight intends to soar
> Above th' *Aonian* Mount, while it pursues
> Things unattempted yet in Prose or Rhime.
>
> (ll. 1–16)

The lines obviously embody one of the precepts of divine poetry as Lily B. Campbell defined it, "a curious balancing of pagan and Christian mythology"; and she herself notes in these lines "the usual opposition of Sion to Olympus, of the dove to Pegasus, of the Christian muse to the pagan muses."[54] To her list I would add that Urania's association with Siloa's brook, however we interpret that body of water, also invites comparison with a pagan parallel alluded to earlier, the mountain spring on Parnassus of which Clio had been the guardian.

Of Clio in this role, Simonides had written:

> She, invoked in many a prayer,
> In robes unwrought with gold,
> For those that came to draw
> Raised from the ambrosial grot
> The fragrant beauteous water.

In quoting this, Plutarch observed that "the cult of the Muses as associates and guardians of the prophetic art" had been established by this very stream and that indeed some believed heroic verse to have been heard there for the first time.[55] At the literal fountainhead of pagan prophecy and heroic poetry, then, stood Clio; and Urania's association with Christian prophecy and poetry, indeed her geographical associations with "*Sion* Hill" and "*Siloa's* Brook that flow'd / Fast by the Oracle of God" all take on greater meaning when measured against the shadowy figure of the now rejected Muse.

Indicative of the high status that Milton gives his poetry is his choice of the word "shepherd" to designate Moses; for although it is accurate in that Moses had been a shepherd (Exodus, chap. 3), it is not so obvious a choice as "leader," "prophet," or "teacher." Its appropriateness becomes apparent when we recall the traditional identification of the shepherd and poet, an identification that Milton had notably exploited in "Lycidas." The poet-shepherd association, further, works in both directions; for it not only associates Moses with poetry, again an association with a scriptural source (Exodus, chap. 15), though an unstressed one, but, more important, associates poetry with the greatest of the Old Testament teacher-prophets. If the Muse of *Paradise Lost* is the same figure who inspired Moses, it is most fitting that she be labeled the sister of Wisdom; and we can expect the poem undertaken under her aegis to partake not at all of the frivolous or worldly.

This the remainder of the prologue confirms. Critics have often noted that the stated intention of the work—

> to soar
> Above th' *Aonian* Mount, while it pursues
> Things unattempted yet in Prose or Rhime—

ironically echoes the opening lines of Ariosto's *Orlando Furioso:*

> Of Dames, of Knights, of armes, of loves delight,
> Of curtesies, of high attempts I speake,
>
> .   .   .   .
>
> I will no lesse *Orlandos* acts declare
> (A tale in prose ne verse yet song or sayd).[56]

In the present study it is worth noting not only how perfectly Ariosto's work embodies the values discussed in the section on Clio, but how clearly its opening places it in the epic tradition. The gloss that accompanied Harington's translation noted this: "This beginning is taken by imitation from Virgil, the I of his Aeneads. Arma virumque cano." Milton then is emphasizing the dissimilarity of his work, not only from Ariosto, but from Virgil as well. He is in fact dismissing the entire epic tradition as built on martial deeds and suggesting that any poet who uses the models, however illustrious, that Ariosto had, cannot succeed as he hopes to.

In rejecting these models, he rejects Clio. It is barely possible, in fact, that the Muse whom Milton dismisses as an empty dream in Book VII, lines 37–39, is Clio, not Calliope, since Clio was sometimes named as Orpheus's mother instead of Calliope.[57] Given his usage of Calliope in the Trinity MS, however, he more likely had her in mind. His slighting references to heroes and deeds of martial valor indicate Clio as his primary target, but his ire is more all-embracing. I stated earlier that with an important caveat, Calliope could be considered the personification of all poetry. That caveat is "all earthly poetry." Because of the tradition that made her the Muse of poetry in general, her dismissal as "an empty dream" underscores, even more than a direct reference to Clio would, the exclusive nature of the poetic concept that Milton invokes.

The exclusiveness of that concept is the theme of the prologue to Book IX. What Milton outlines in Book I, he now fills in with emphatic detail. Once again he compares his work with earlier epics, including the *Aeneid*, the *Iliad*, and the *Odyssey* (lines 13–19), to stress his conviction that the Fall of Adam and Eve constitutes a more genuinely heroic subject than the action of these epics. Once chosen, his subject ensured the nightly visitation of his "Celestial Patroness," but this began only when he had rejected what can fairly be called the material of Clio—

> Races and Games,
> Or tilting Furniture, emblazon'd Shields,
> Impreses quaint, Caparisons and Steeds;
> Bases and tinsel Trappings, gorgious Knights
> At Joust and Torneament; then marshal'd Feast
> Serv'd up in Hall with Sewers and Seneshals—

all of which he dismisses as "Not that which justly gives Heroic name / To Person or to Poem" (lines 33–41).

Without Urania's aid, all human poetry (Calliope) becomes hopelessly inadequate, especially the heroic poetry he had aspired to write under the aegis of Clio. With Urania's aid, all things poetic once again become possible; the Christian artist is able to do the work that God has set for him. Appropriately for a votary of Urania, he must give up his own inclinations. His times, the climate, old age, his own abilities and efforts even, all these may hinder him in the completion of his work "if all be mine, / Not Hers who brings it nightly to my Ear" (IX, 46–47). Such is the "Heav'nly Muse," Urania, Christian, renunciatory, and antithetically opposed to all that had previously been considered heroic in poetry.

Obviously, a parallel can be drawn between Milton's conception of his task as Musal amanuensis and his conception of heroism as bodied forth in Adam. Both concepts are in a sense passive. Milton expends far less effort in the writing of his greatest work than he had planned on; Adam achieves heroic stature with the expenditure of far less energy in doing big things than his epic predecessors. But it is passivity with a difference. The willingness to do God's will, however slight seemingly its manifestations, is the generative action that makes all the difference between the deeds and poetry of the fallen angels in Book II and the poetry and deeds of *Paradise Lost* itself.

To conclude, Urania summarizes how and what Milton wrote. Obviously, very little of what went into her was original with him. This would have been even more obvious to his audience, which shared his intellectual background, than it is to us who have painstakingly to reconstruct that background. Indeed, the pains we must take encourage us to fall into another trap, that of emphasizing the abstruseness of the materials out of which his Muse is constituted. Milton, however, is not abstruse. He is not even learned on the ground merely that he knew Spenser or Du Bartas or, for that matter, Macrobius or Simonides. Most of his audience knew these writers, if not directly, at least through the medium of the ever so common handbooks and dictionaries examined here. He is learned rather because he had mastered, in every sense of the word, the authors he studied. With ever-increasing ease, he knew when and why and how to use his sources. With regard to Urania, this means he evaluated each source in the light of his experience in writing his poem and the values he wished it to embody. If my sketch of how he composed *Paradise Lost* is right, the evaluations were by now largely subconscious; but they had behind them a rigorous education and a lifetime of writing according to highly conscious, eminently articulable principles. Steeping ourselves in that education, those principles, we come a little better to appreciate his achievement: a Muse who is no labored and bookish pastiche, but a mysterious and living presence.

6

In His Blindness Seeing All

FOR A twentieth-century scholar, the seventeenth-century educational system is apt to seem incredibly rigid, prescriptive, and dull. For Milton, however much he may have disliked certain aspects of it, it was finally a beneficent influence. By teaching essentially the same materials to all, it served as an effective bonding agent between him and his audience, and its ability to function thus for so original a writer as Milton is not irrelevant to consideration of public issues that are still very much with us. More important yet are the ways his education encouraged him to incorporate the voices of the past into his own voice, for study of these ways sheds a modicum of light on what is after all the most fascinating of mysteries, the act of artistic creation.

So far as Milton and his original audience were concerned, their preferences among authors, their interpretations of *exempla* might differ, but Milton and his readers—Protestant and Catholic, Puritan and Cavalier—had been taught the same writers in the same way. He therefore did not have the problem of constructing his own literary milieu or communicating its fruits to a fragmented audience, few of whom could be counted on to share or comprehend that self-constructed environment. That Milton's audience could quickly grasp the common materials out of which Urania had been drawn meant that it could also grasp the uncommon skill with which she had been fashioned.

At first glance, then, it might seem that the moral of the

story is that a return to a more uniform curriculum and to more rigorous methods of teaching might assist today's poets by creating larger and more understanding communities of readers to share their work; and indeed every newspaper, magazine, and professional journal we pick up contains discussion of some such proposal. The question of a canon for American schools, for example, is still very much alive. Some of our century's most penetrating and liberal minds have concluded, as George Santayana observed decades ago, "that it did not matter, in education, what books were read so long as everybody read the same books," and the proposals in recent years of the Paideia group suggest that for some acute observers of our current educational scene, this sentiment still seems viable and desirable.[1] This study of Milton does not mean that we necessarily endorse without question *The Paideia Proposal;* for history here as always teaches through stimulating an awareness of the differences as well as the similarities of the past to the present. Hard questions have to be asked, such as how any canon, whatever its contents, can be squared with the ethnic and ideological multiplicity of our society or the multifarious ends that education now must serve. The practical application of this study, then, is limited, and yet final judgment is to some extent tempered by the knowledge that authors benefit when they can work with a sure sense of what is fair to expect in the way of audience knowledge.

Unrelated to matters of public policy, yet ultimately more significant to us as students of literature is the effect that Milton's education had on his relation to earlier writers. The thoroughness with which he studied the classical authors, the exhaustively articulated principles of composition, the years of practice gave him a command over the past that most of today's authors can only envy. His education, however, does not explain the completeness with which he made the past his own, and it is that dimension of his art that makes him peculiarly relevant and yet irrelevant to our own day; for poets living in the chaos of today's world must ponder not only how to communicate with the few readers they have, but also how to nourish their souls so that they can write at all. Their stance—like Milton's and unlike the great apostles of Modernism—is

In His Blindness Seeing All

to adapt the work of kindred spirits to the insistent needs of their own strongly felt personalities. One of the best among them, Robert Duncan, has located his origins as a poet in high-school exercises not all that different from the ones in *imitatio* that Milton himself did. At first, it sounds as if the writers whom he imitated powerfully affected him in that they enabled him to get outside himself, to find, that is, an objective tradition into which he could fit:

> What really got me ... was the practice of imitating poems in class. When we read Chaucer, we read the Prologue and then we wrote prologues ourselves to an imaginary pilgrimage poem. And then when we came to Robert Browning we wrote dramatic monologues, and there I discovered another thing that I had always loved, and that was "being" throughout the period of mankind. And Robert Browning suddenly showed you that you could go into words and be all sorts of people. And that was so exciting that then I knew I wasn't going to be an architect; I was going to be a poet.[2]

As he continues, however, it becomes clear that the significance of these exercises for him did not at all lie in their taking him out of himself, but rather in his finding himself powerfully embodied in these earlier authors:

> So one of the discoveries is to discover a kindred poet, and to learn to write like him. That's your master; you don't study in a classroom with him. It's entirely voluntary. Blake recognized in Milton his master and that he was his antitype. To be a true son means that you are the antitype of your father and then you know that you belong to a generative order. And your spirit awakens to it. But at first it awakens only along the lines of admiration or the feeling of a power, or the feeling of wanting to *be* like that, and you go into it spiritually, and that means to write like it, to learn to write like it.[3]

Milton, I think, would have agreed with this. Most of the authors we have discussed were authors whom he learned about in school; some, such as Spenser, were not. And if we can accept Dryden's reporting as accurate, he seems to have referred to this relation in ways very similar to Duncan's own words: "*Milton* was the Poetical Son of *Spencer,* and . . . has acknowledg'd to me, that *Spencer* was his Original."4 Even with regard to the authors he did study in school, however, his response was still very different from that of his peers, most of whom would probably have subscribed to Adam Martindale's description of his schoolboy exercises as following Cicero, "though (alas!) at a great distance."5 As I stated at the outset, to say that these writers were Milton's friends is to imply a greater distance than in fact existed. He simply incorporated them into himself and thought no more about using them. They became as much a part of him as the food we eat becomes a part of our own bodies so that to speak of him as using them is in a sense misleading. He has so adapted them to himself that one might more accurately speak of his using himself, his own inner resources, as of his using external sources in the form of earlier authors.

To what extent did the system in which he trained contribute to his greatness? Possibly its very strength encouraged him to utilize it through incorporation rather than rebellion. Certainly we can say that similarly spirited writers of our own century have found that their use of the past is a source of greater tension and frustration than Milton's was. With Milton, they share a desire to use the past on their own terms, responding warmly to his strong feeling that "whatever is right and laudable in [my work], that same I shall seem not more to have derived from authors of high excellence than to have fetched forth pure and sincere from the inmost feelings of my own mind and soul."6 The modern poet cannot in any sense, however, approximate the fusion of "authors of high excellence" and "inmost feelings" that Milton accomplished.

For those who write today, then, Milton serves both as a powerful and attractive example and also as a poignant reminder of their own exigent problems. Obviously, the Miltonic attitude stated above did not endear him to writers such as T. S. Eliot who felt that poetry should be "not the expression of personality, but an escape from personality."7 Obviously, too, it is the same quality that has endeared him to writers such as Duncan and Ginsberg, who seek frankly to express themselves in their work and who, like Milton, wish no separation of response between their work and themselves. With sufficient distance, we can see that no poet, not even Eliot, completely abstracts himself from his work. Indeed, James E. Miller, Jr. has demonstrated with great acuity just how personal a poem *The Waste Land* is.[8] Nevertheless, a profound shift in emphasis has occurred in the last forty years; and it is this shift that explains the tremendous difference in tone separating Eliot's grudging admiration from Ginsberg's handsome tribute to "Milton dwelling as in a starry temple / brooding in his blindness seeing all" (*Collected Poems*, p. 164).

If, however, we carefully examine contemporary treatments of creativity—whether traditional ones such as John Fowles's *Mantissa* or Romantic ones such as Ginsberg's "Blessed be the Muses" and "Contest of Bards"—we begin to understand something of the burden that dessicated tradition and ambivalence toward the past impose on today's artists. Two of these works, *Mantissa* and "Blessed be the Muses," specifically employ the Muses, an act that immediately involves their authors in difficulties not faced by Milton; for since the eighteenth century it has been felt that the Muses, except in rare instances, are no longer appropriate for inclusion in serious poetry. Coleridge, for example, tells us that his headmaster at Christ Hospital, the Reverend Boyer, held firmly to the view that their overuse had for the most part already invalidated their usage:

> In our own English compositions . . . he showed no mercy to phrase, metaphor, or image, unsupported by a sound sense, or where the same sense might have been conveyed with equal force and dignity in plainer words. Lute, harp, and lyre, muse, muses, and inspirations, Pegasus, Parnassus, and Hippocrene were all an abomination to him. In fancy I can almost hear him now, exclaiming *"Harp? Harp? Lyre? Pen and ink, boy, you mean! Muse, boy, muse? Your Nurse's daughter, you mean! Pierian spring? Oh, aye! the cloister pump, I suppose!"*[9]

Since that time, the Muses have for the most part been limited in serious poetry to the satirical, as in Lord Byron's "Hail, Muse! *et cetera,*" or the elegiac, exemplified in Edwin Arlington Robinson's lament:

> Oh for a poet—for a beacon bright
> To rift this changless glimmer of dead gray;
> To spirit back the Muses, long astray,
> And flush Parnassus with a newer light.[10]

For Fowles, then, to make a Muse into a principal character in his novel, *Mantissa,* is immediately to signal that he aims not so much to create the illusion of life in his work as to call attention to its being a consciously artistic construct. Purporting to chronicle the stormy relations between a beleaguered novelist, Miles Green, and his hopelessly uncooperative Muse, Erato, who has appropriately annexed all of prose fiction to her original domain of love poetry, the novel's scene is the author's mind; its characters, different facets of that same mind; and none of it, he continually reminds us, relates at all to anything outside that mind. "Serious modern fiction," he assures his Muse, "has only one subject: the difficulty of writing serious modern fiction. First, it has fully accepted that it is only fiction, can only be fiction, will never be anything but fiction, and therefore has no business at all tampering with real life or reality."[11] Green—and Fowles, unless the novel is designed as an object lesson in what not to do—thus joins hands with a distinguished company of twentieth-century authors—Borges, Robbe-Grillet, Nathalie Saurraute, for example—whose work has been interpreted as signifying that our culture is so near its end that authors can continue to function only by making the accumulated intellectual capital of the past their subject rather than their means of writing about the questions and answers that are always worth writing about.

The more Romantic of our writers such as Ginsberg continue a more hopeful search for fresh ways of writing about the old problems. In one instance, a very short poem whose title serves as its first line, he even manages to bring the Muses alive in a manner neither satirical nor elegiac:

In His Blindness Seeing All

> Blessed be the Muses
> for their descent,
> dancing round my desk,
> crowning my balding head
> with Laurel.
> (*Collected Poems,* p. 125)

One might argue that the details of the desk and the poet's balding head so ill assort with the implied traditional picture of the young shepherd-poet piping in the meadows that the poem is satirical. This argument is vitiated, however, by Ginsberg's characteristic insistence that we accept him as he is, including those facets of his person that are ridiculous or even offensive, or give up reading him altogether. Acceptance on Ginsberg's terms means then that here we see the balding poet sitting at his desk not as a faintly ridiculous figure, but rather as a heroic one, not young, nor particularly attractive, yet bold to claim that the Muses, present in all their authority, mystery, and grace, have found him an apt recipient of their gifts.

Aware perhaps that the Muses can maintain that authority, mystery, and grace only when glimpsed briefly, Ginsberg avoided them in his 1977 poem, "Contest of Bards," his most significant exploration of creativity and the author's relation to the past (*Collected Poems,* pp. 665–79). At a minimum, "Contest of Bards" suggests that Ginsberg accedes neither to cultural moribundity nor to the drastic diminution in artistic significance that *Mantissa* involves. If, on reflection, it proves more problematic in evaluation than the Miltonic work examined here, part of the difficulty lies in a literary milieu that gives its authors little of the support that Milton's gave him and part lies in the greater strength of character that enabled him more calmly to appropriate the past.

One's first impression, however, is favorable. Ginsberg has replaced the Muses with figures who are part bard and part shaman to convey the struggle involved in writing, particularly as it involves the utilization of the past. The homosexual act that occurs between the old, bearded bard and the beautiful young poet, the older using the younger's "form as a girl," is the means whereby wisdom and tradition are transmitted from one generation to another; but the matter is more complicated than that, for the older man is not all-wise nor the younger all-passive. Indeed, as the title indicates, the younger poet is also a bard, seeking not only to be instructed but to instruct; nor is the relationship between them one only of love and mutual enrichment. Anger and mutual recrimination also are present, and it is out of the clash and ambiguity of their exchanges that Ginsberg seeks to create a memorable image of both the pain and pleasure the poet experiences in making the past a vital element in his work.

The desire not passively to receive the past, but to interact with it in creating one's own voice is Miltonic; the anger and mutual recrimination, if I am right, are not. If I read correctly the relation between Milton and the materials he learned in school and on his own, my own images—the metaphor of incorporation, which emphasizes the impossibility of distinguishing between what was formerly separate; the paradox of Milton's simultaneous originality and unoriginality—most illuminate the process that occurred. If he was happier in the possession of a stable and ubiquitous tradition than today's poets, he was also a greater poet. The statements above are of course controversial. Critics of Freudian and deconstructive orientation see Milton's relation to the past as stormier and more problematic than I do. "Contest of Bards," in my view, illustrates "the anxiety of influence" better by far than Milton's own work; and yet Harold Bloom's most famous pronouncement, that Milton constitutes the central problem for any theory of influence in modern English poetry, is entirely correct, its correctness validated among other ways by the tremendous number of recent studies that investigate different facets of Milton's relations to earlier writers and traditions.[12] Almost all these studies involve a significant rethinking of what is meant by source study. What need was there, for example, for Richard DuRocher to remap Milton's relation to Ovid when Mary Campbell Brill neatly tallied up all the verbal correspondences over fifty years ago?[13] Great need, because we recognize now that influence itself is a more mysterious matter than any bookkeeping approach, however systematic and thorough, can indicate.

Even in the seventeenth century, aided by a ubiquitous and thoroughly taught tradition, Milton's making the past Miltonic was a spectacular triumph. Like all such triumphs, it is not reproducible and therefore not entirely relevant to the present. We cannot restore life to worn-out traditions by continuing to write in them; we cannot erase hostility, whether directed toward our natural or our literary fathers, by denying that it exists. On the other hand, it is crystal clear that Milton is not nearly so irrelevant as was thought not so many years ago. So long as there are poets who do not accede to our culture's death and seek to use the past; so long as there are critics who strive to understand that usage, Milton impinges on our consciousness at every turn. He speaks to us of gain and loss, of what we now are and of what we would be.

NOTES

1. Tradition and the Individual Talent

1. "On Shakespeare and Milton" in *The Complete Works*, ed. P. P. Howe, V (London: J. M. Dent, 1930), 58.

2. *Images and Themes in Five Poems by Milton* (Cambridge, Mass.: Harvard University Press, 1957), p. 5.

3. *Urbane Milton: The Latin Poetry*, guest eds. James A. Freeman and Anthony Low, *Milton Studies*, 19 (1984), x.

4. Respectively Christopher Hill, *Milton and the English Revolution* (London: Faber and Faber, 1977); Joan Webber, "Walking on Water: Milton, Stevens, and Contemporary Poetry," in *Milton and the Line of Vision*, ed. Joseph Anthony Wittreich, Jr. (Madison: University of Wisconsin Press, 1975), pp. 231–68; Herman Rapaport, *Milton and the Postmodern* (Lincoln and London: University of Nebraska Press, 1983).

5. See R. M. Frazer's recent translation of *The Poems of Hesiod* (Norman: University of Oklahoma Press, 1983), pp. 23–30.

6. *The Origin of Consciousness in the Breakdown of the Bicameral Mind* (Boston: Houghton Mifflin, 1976), p. 371.

7. "Phaedrus" in *The Collected Dialogues of Plato*, ed. Edith Hamilton and Huntington Cairns, Bollingen Series, No. 71 (New York: Pantheon Books, 1961), p. 492.

8. *Tusculan Disputations*, V, 23, trans. J. E. King, Loeb Classical Library (Cambridge, Mass.: Harvard University Press, 1945), 5: 492–93.

9. *On Christian Doctrine*, 2, xviii, trans. D. W. Robertson, Library of Liberal Arts (Indianapolis: Bobbs-Merrill, 1958), p. 54. On the rejection of the Muses by late classical, Christian poets, see Ernst Robert Curtius, *European Literature and the Latin Middle Ages*, trans. Willard R. Trask (New York: Harper and Row, 1953), p. 235. Curtius's chapter on "The Muses," pp. 228–46, condenses two earlier studies that appeared in *Zeitschrift für Romanische Philologie*, 59 (1939), 129–88, and 63 (1943), 256–68. For the period that these earlier studies cover (the Augustan Age to ca. 1100) they are still the most comprehensive survey of Muse lore undertaken.

10. Edward Phillips, "The Life of Mr. John Milton," 1694, in *The Early Lives of Milton,* ed. Helen Darbishire (London: Constable, 1932), p. 72, hereafter cited as *Early Lives.*

11. Virtually every Miltonist who has written on *Paradise Lost:* A. W. Verity, E. M. W. Tillyard, Maurice Kelley, James Holly Hanford, Merritt Y. Hughes, Dame Helen Gardner, for example, has added to that commentary. Specific treatments that have appeared in the last twenty years include Harry F. Robins, *If This Be Heresy: A Study of Milton and Origen*, Illinois Studies in Language and Literature no. 51 (Urbana: University of Illinois Press, 1963), Chap. 5, "Milton's Muse," pp. 157–75; William B. Hunter, Jr., "Milton's Urania," *Studies in English Literature* 4 (Winter 1964), 35–42; revised in *Bright Essence: Studies in Milton's Theology,* ed. William B. Hunter, Jr., C. A. Patrides, J. H. Adamson (Salt Lake City: University of Utah Press, 1971), pp. 149–56; Nathaniel Henry, "The Mystery of Milton's Muse," *Renaissance Papers* 12 (1967), 69–83; Naseeb Shaheen, "Milton's Muse and the *De Doctrina,*" *Milton Quarterly* 3 (October 1974), 72–76.

12. Lawrence Jay Dessner, *How to Write a Poem* (New York: Washington Mews Books, 1979), p. 164.

13. *The First Defence of the English People,* in *The Works of John Milton,* ed. Frank Allen Patterson et al. (New York: Columbia University Press, 1931–38), 7: 66–67. Hereafter CM.

14. Cornell Studies in English (New Haven: Yale University Press, 1924), p. 60.

15. *An Apology against a Pamphlet* (CM, 3: 303).

16. Milton to Emeric Bigot, March 24, 1656 (CM, 12: 85–87).

17. *Milton: A Biography* (Oxford: Clarendon Press, 1968), Vol. I, p. vii.

18. *John Milton: Englishman* (New York: Crown, 1949), p. 264.

19. *Collected Poems, 1947–1980* (New York: Harper and Row, 1984), pp. 163–64. The date of Ginsberg's poem, "POEM Rocket," October 4, 1957, indicates how long ago the change described got under way.

20. Mary Ann Radzinowicz, *Toward "Samson Agonistes": The Growth of Milton's Mind* (Princeton: Princeton University Press, 1978); William Kerrigan, *The Sacred Complex: On the Psychogenesis of Paradise Lost* (Cambridge, Mass.: Harvard University Press, 1983).

21. Joseph Anthony Wittreich, Jr., *Visionary Poetics: Milton's Tradition and His Legacy* (San Marino: Huntington Library, 1979); John Guillory, *Poetic Authority: Spenser, Milton, and Literary History* (New York: Columbia University Press, 1983); Maureen Quilligan, *Milton's Spenser: The Politics of Reading* (Ithaca: Cornell University Press, 1983); Richard J. DuRocher, *Milton and Ovid* (Ithaca: Cornell University Press, 1985); Paul Stevens, *Imagination and the Presence of Shakespeare in Paradise Lost* (Madison: University of Wisconsin Press, 1985).

22. On the varying quality of "imitation," see Chap. 2 "Schooling and Approaches to Theory," in Ruth Wallerstein's *Studies in Seventeenth-Century Poetic* (Madison: University of Wisconsin Press, 1950), pp. 11–58; Thomas M. Greene, *The Light in Troy: Imitation and Discovery in Renaissance Poetry* (New Haven: Yale University Press, 1982); and G. W. Pigman III, "Versions of Imitation in the Renaissance," *Renaissance Quarterly* 33 (Spring 1980), 1–32.

23. "Elegy 4," ll. 29–32 (CM, 1: 186–87). See Chapter 5 below for specific discussion of this passage. Documentary evidence for when Young was Milton's tutor is lacking, and the precise facts alluded to in this passage are not clear.

24. Dell's comments appeared in *The Right Reformation of Learning, Schools, and Universities* (1653) and are quoted in Kenneth Charlton, "The Educational Background," *The Age of*

Notes to Chapter 2

Milton, ed. C. A. Patrides and Raymond B. Waddington (Manchester: Manchester University Press, 1980), p. 103.

25. Hobbes's cool evaluation of the Muses' place in modern literature appears in his "Answer to the Preface to Gondibert," in *The English Works of Thomas Hobbes*, ed. Sir William Molesworth (1840; reprint ed., Darmstadt: Scientia Verlag Aalen, 1966), 4: 447–48.

2. THE TENDER STOPS OF VARIOUS QUILLS

1. I, 201–204 (CM, 2: 412).

2. J. Milton French provides the data for this statement in *Life Records of John Milton* (New Brunswick: Rutgers University Press, 1958), 5: 154, 157–58. The poet's mother must have been born by February 11, 1573, when she was mentioned in an uncle's will and was therefore around thirty-six at the time of his birth. French is not so definite on the age of Milton's father; but Parker, through lynx-eyed scrutiny of French's materials, establishes that he was born in the last three months of 1562 and was thus forty-six when his son was born (*Milton*, vol. II, pp. 684–85). On the death of an older brother or sister, see French, 5: 173.

3. Milton's father was a musician of some ability. His music was published in a number of contemporary collections, the most famous of which was Thomas Morley's *Madrigals* of 1601 (French, 5: 170–71). The story of the father's disinheritance for Protestantism and subsequently making his way as a scrivener is well known. French gives the bare facts (5: 163–70); Ernest Brennecke, Jr., *John Milton the Elder and His Music*, Columbia University Studies in Musicology, no. 2 (New York: Columbia University Press, 1938), attempts to clothe them in significance. While one may deplore Brennecke's lack of critical rigor, his impulse surely was right.

4. Authority for this lies in Milton's own statement in *Reason of Church-Government* about "the Church, to whose service by the intentions of my parents and friends I was destin'd of a child" (CM, 3: 242), supplemented by numerous comments in his own writings and the early biographers as to the ample and thorough nature of his education.

5. Diodati to Milton, Spring 1626 (CM, 12: 295).
6. September [November?] 2, 1637 (CM, 12: 19).
7. September [November?] 23, 1637 (CM, 12: 29).
8. The earliest extant curriculum for St. Paul's was prepared by Thomas Gale, High Master, 1672–97. It is reproduced in Donald Lemen Clark, *John Milton at St. Paul's School* (New York: Columbia University Press, 1948; reprint ed. Archon Books, 1964), pp. 110–13. It refers to "turning verses and proving them" in the fourth year, a practice that T. W. Baldwin describes as "preparatory to beginning composition in verse in the fifth form" (*William Shakspere's Small Latine & Lesse Greeke* [Urbana: University of Illinois Press, 1944], 1: 120). Charles Hoole, whose *New Discovery of the Old Art of Teaching Schoole* is a very full contemporary account of pedagogical practice, had his fourth-year students not only turn and prove verses but actually begin writing English verse, though strictly as preparation for the writing of Latin verse. See the edition of E. T. Campagnac (Liverpool: The University Press, 1913), "The Master's Method," pp. 157–58. In terms of norms, then, Milton's being a poet at age ten was a bit unusual.
9. John Aubrey in *Early Lives,* p. 10. The anonymous biographer (John Phillips? Cyriac Skinner?) also mentions Milton's "indefatigable industry (sitting up constantly at his Study till midnight)" and his early compositions (*Early Lives,* p. 18).
10. "De Ratione Studii," in *Desiderius Erasmus concerning the Aim and Method of Education,* Classics in Education, no. 19 (1904; reprint ed., New York: Bureau of Publications, Teachers College, Columbia University, 1964), pp. 162–63.
11. "Of Education," CM, 4: 277.
12. The distinguished historian of education, Foster Watson, has written of the classical curriculum as practiced in English schools over several centuries: "The aim of the schools was not so much humanistic, in the sense of imparting a training in literature, as it was practical, in attempting to give the pupils control over the instrument of all culture of their own and preceding ages. Roman and Greek literature were studied not so much as ends in themselves as the storehouses of adequate and eloquent expression, the happy hunting-ground of

the right thing to discourse about, and the right way of saying it." See Watson's *The English Grammar Schools to 1660* (1908; reprint ed., New York: Augustus M. Kelley, 1970), pp. 5–6.

13. The happiest exposition of those activities for Milton remains Clark's *Milton at St. Paul's*. The most exhaustive exposition of the English school system in the 16th and 17th centuries is contained in two monumental studies by T. W. Baldwin—*William Shakspere's Petty School* (Urbana: University of Illinois Press, 1943) and *William Shakspere's Small Latine & Lesse Greeke*. Of varied quality are a number of other works relating to Milton's education both at St. Paul's and Cambridge: Ruth M. Baldwin, "Alexander Gill, the Elder, High Master of St. Paul's School: An Approach to Milton's Intellectual Development," Ph.D. diss., University of Illinois, 1955; Arthur Barker, "Milton's Schoolmasters," *Modern Language Review* 32 (October 1937), 517–36; Eugenia Chifos, "Alexander Gill," M.A. thesis, Ohio State University, 1945; Clark, "John Milton and William Chappell," *Huntington Library Quarterly* 18 (August 1955), 329–50; William T. Costello, S.J., *The Scholastic Curriculum at Early Seventeenth-Century Cambridge* (Cambridge, Mass.: Harvard University Press, 1958); Harris F. Fletcher, *The Intellectual Development of John Milton*, Vol. 1, *The Institution to 1625: From the Beginnings through Grammar School* (1956); Vol. 2, *The Cambridge University Period, 1625–1632* (Urbana: University of Illinois Press, 1961); Davis P. Harding, *Milton and the Renaissance Ovid*, Illinois Studies in Language and Literature 30, no. 4 (Urbana: University of Illinois Press, 1946); A. F. Leach, "Milton as Schoolboy and Schoolmaster," *Proceedings of the British Academy*, 3 (1907–08), 295–318; W. Arthur Turner, "The Known English Acquaintances of John Milton," Ph.D. diss., Ohio State University, 1947.

14. *The Life of Adam Martindale, Written by Himself,* ed. Richard Parkinson, Chetham Society Publications 4 (Manchester: Charles Simms, 1845), p. 15.

15. *New Discovery,* "The Usher's Duty," p. 14. Hoole's work divides into four treatises: "The Petty-Schoole," "The Usher's Duty," "The Masters Method," and "Scholastick Discipline." Since the first section is numbered separately from the others,

necessity dictates naming the treatise in which each quotation is included.

16. Milton's correspondence with Young includes two letters (CM, 12: 4–7; 12–15), possibly the "Letter to a Friend," (CM, 12: 320–25), and "Elegy 4," (CM, 1: 184–95). His three letters to Gill appear in CM, 12: 6–13, and 14–17. On the date of the first one, see Chifos, "Milton's Letter to Gill, May 20, 1628," *MLN* 62 (January 1947), 37–39. For Gill's possible influence on "Ad Patrem," see Marguerite Little, "Milton's Ad Patrem and the Younger Gill's In Natalem Mei Parentis," *Journal of English and Germanic Philology* 49 (July 1950), 345–51. See also the items by Barker and Chifos cited above in n. 13.

17. In addition to the comments of Hoole quoted above, see John Brinsley on the same point and on the value of understanding what one learned (*Ludus Literarius*, ed. Campagnac [Liverpool: The University Press, 1917], pp. 5ff. and 41ff.)

18. Fletcher, who has done the most with the texts Milton used or may have used, notes that "unfortunately there is no surviving edition of Lily's grammar bearing a date that exactly fits the time when Milton began his formal study of Latin, perhaps about 1615" (*Intellectual Development*, 1: 133). So far as I can tell, the use of *musa, -ae* as the first-declension noun remained constant. Two modern facsimiles to illustrate are those of Vincent J. Flynn (New York: Scholars' Facsimiles & Reprints, 1945) of the edition of 1567; and the Scolar Press facs. of the 1549 edition (Menston, England, 1970). Other citations, which establish that this was the commonly used noun, appear in Hoole, "The Usher's Duty," p. 19; Brinsley, pp. 58–59; and Milton's own "Accidence Commenc't Grammar," CM, 6: 291.

19. For the various meanings that Milton assigned to the word, see the material from Walter MacKellar's edition of the Latin poems, cited in n. 29 below.

20. Third edition (London, 1559). An augmentation of Sir Thomas Elyot's *Dictionary* of 1538, Cooper's work both as *Bibliotheca Eliotae* and after 1565 as *Thesaurus Linguae Romanae et Britannicae* was very popular. On the books at St. Paul's in the 16th and 17th centuries, see Robert B. Gardiner, *The Admission Registers of St. Paul's School* (London: George Bell, 1884), app. I, "The School Library," pp. 452–53.

Notes to Chapter 2

21. According to the Gale MS, the *Colloquies* were taught there in the later 17th century, and Clark includes them in his conjectured curriculum of Paul's for the years Milton was there (*Milton at St. Paul's*, pp. 111, 121). The Gale MS, "The constant Method of Teaching in St. Pauls Schoole London," was prepared by Thomas Gale. The Erasmian *Colloquies* were included by him in third-year materials.

22. *Le Banquet Poétique*, ed. Verdun L. Saulnier (Melun: Librairie D'Argences, 1948), p. 28. The English translation is that of Craig R. Thompson, who has done all the *Colloquies* into English (Chicago: University of Chicago Press, 1965), p. 160.

23. *Metamorphoses*, ed. Karl K. Hulley and Stanley T. Vandersall (Lincoln: University of Nebraska Press, 1970), pp. 247–48.

24. *Bibliotheca Eliotae*. Subsequent editions differ only in incidentals of spelling and punctuation.

25. Paris, 1553. My translation.

26. Lyons, 1573. My translation.

27. Trans. Arthur Leslie Wheeler, Loeb Classical Library (Cambridge, Mass.: Harvard University Press, 1965), pp. 2–3.

28. Joannes Buchler, *Sacrarum Profanarumque Phraseum Poeticarum Thesaurus* (London, 1632), pp. 78–79 (*Early English Books, 1475–1640,* University Microfilm, Reel 1299).

29. Cornell Studies in English, no. 15 (New Haven: Yale University Press, 1930), p. 193.

30. Douglas Bush rejects as implausible the suggestion of G. M. Gathorne-Hardy that *destin'd Urn* is "the memorial I am now, under inspiration of the Muses, preparing for Lycidas" and *he* is "Lycidas" (*A Variorum Commentary on the Poems of John Milton* [New York: Columbia University Press, 1972], 2: 646). The image of Lycidas turning within the urn Milton has prepared for him to bid fair peace to Milton's sable shroud does indeed seem a strained reading of the lines.

31. MacKellar's reference is to "To Salsilli," l. 1—"O Musa gressum quae volens trahis claudum"—where the "limping Muse" refers to the limping effect of the scazontic meter in which the poem is written.

32. CM, 12: 138–39, ll. 12–16.

33. Quoted in Fletcher, *Intellectual Development*, 2: 637.

34. *Institutio Oratoria* (10.2) in *Ancient Literary Criticism*, eds. D. A. Russell and Michael Winterbottom (Oxford: Clarendon Press, 1972), p. 403.

35. Cited in Watson, *English Grammar Schools*, pp. 465–466.

36. *The Miltonic Setting* (London: Chatto and Windus, 1938), p. 20.

37. Cicero to Lentulus, I, ix, trans. W. Glynn Williams, Loeb Classical Library (Cambridge, Mass.: Harvard University Press, 1927), 82–83.

38. *Small Latine*, 1: 305, 310, 417, 314, 430–31, 750.

39. *Life of Adam Martindale*, p. 14.

40. *Milton at St. Paul's*, p. 121.

3. THE MELLOWING YEAR

1. Quoted in Foster Watson, *The English Grammar Schools* (1908; reprint ed., New York: Augustus M. Kelley, 1970), p. 466.

2. "Wine, Poetry, and Milton's Elegia Sexta," *English Studies* 21 (1939), 164–65.

3. *Mystagogus Poeticus, or The Muses Interpreter*, 2d ed. (London, 1648), p. 298.

4. *Complete Poetry of Ben Jonson*, ed. William B. Hunter, Jr. (Garden City: Doubleday, 1963), p. 376.

5. For full citations to Latin writers, see Charlton T. Lewis and Charles Short, eds., *A Latin Dictionary* (Oxford: Clarendon Press, 1879), s.v. "Camena."

6. Ll. 168–78 (CM, 1: 312–13).

7. See the entries on "Camenae" in Samuel Ball Platner and Thomas Ashby, eds., *A Topographical Dictionary of Ancient Rome* (Oxford: Oxford University Press, 1929) and in *The Oxford Classical Dictionary*, 2d ed., ed. N. G. L. Hammond and H. H. Scullard (Oxford: Clarendon Press, 1970).

8. *From the Founding of the City*, I, xviii–xxi, Loeb Classical Library, trans. B. O. Foster (Cambridge, Mass.: Harvard University Press, 1919), 1: 64–65.

9. Ll. 12–20, in *Juvenal and Persius*, Loeb Classical Library,

trans. G. G. Ramsay (Cambridge, Mass.: Harvard University Press, 1940), pp. 32–33.

10. Bk. 8, chap. 3, Loeb Classical Library, trans. Frank Granger (Cambridge, Mass.: Harvard University Press, 1934), 2: 150–51.

11. Bk. 7, sec. 27, Loeb Classical Library, trans. Roland G. Kent (Cambridge, Mass.: Harvard University Press, 1951), 1: 294–95.

12. My translation, s.v. "Camoenae" from the *Dictionarium* (Paris, 1553).

13. Virgil, Eclogue 8, l. 70, Loeb Classical Library, rev. ed., trans. H. Rushton Fairclough (Cambridge, Mass.: Harvard University Press, 1934), 1: 60–61; Horace, Epode 17, l. 4, Loeb Classical Library, rev. ed., trans. C. E. Bennett (Cambridge, Mass.: Harvard University Press, 1927), pp. 408–409. See the entry on "carmen" in Lewis and Short for numerous examples of this usage.

14. My translation, s.v. "Camoenae" (Lyons, 1573).

15. *Tusculan Disputations*, II, xv, trans. J. E. King, Loeb Classical Library (Cambridge, Mass.: Harvard University Press, 1945), pp. 182–83.

16. Satire 6, ll. 286–305, *Juvenal and Persius*, pp. 106–107.

17. Life of Numa (sec. 13) in the *Lives*, trans. Bernadotte Perrin, Loeb Classical Library (Cambridge, Mass.: Harvard University Press, 1914), 1: 350–51.

18. *Remains of Old Latin*, trans. E. H. Warmington, Loeb Classical Library (Cambridge, Mass.: Harvard University Press, 1936), 2: 24–25.

19. Third ed. (London, 1559), s.v. "Camoenae."

20. Review of E. M. W. Tillyard, *The Miltonic Setting*, in *MLN* 55 (March 1940), 215–18; *Milton*, pp. 67–70.

21. *Variorum Commentary*, 1: 112–14. Among earlier scholars who interpreted the poem autobiographically, Bush mentions A. S. P. Woodhouse, David Masson, James Holly Hanford, and Tillyard. Masson, for example, wrote that ll. 55–78 express "an eminently Miltonic idea, perhaps *pre*-eminently *the* Miltonic idea" and adds that "these twenty-four lines are about Milton's noblest in Latin, and deserve to be learnt by heart

Notes to Chapter 3

with reference to himself, or to be written under his portrait" (*Poetical Works of John Milton* [London: Macmillan, 1882], 1: 93). Anthony Low, who has more recently examined the poem, concludes that "it reflects Milton's serious dedication to his poetic career" ("The Unity of Milton's *Elegia Sexta*," *English Literary Renaissance* 11 [Spring 1981], 223).

22. Godfrey Davies, *The Early Stuarts*, 2d ed. (London: Oxford University Press for Readers Union, 1964), pp. 304–305.

23. Bush, 1: 115, note to ll. 6–8.

24. *Collected Dialogues of Plato*, p. 220. For undergraduate references to Plato, see Elegy 4, 23–24 (CM, 1: 186–87); "De Idea Platonica quemadmodum Aristoteles intellexit" (CM, 12: 218–19, 238–39); "Il Penseroso," ll. 87–96 (CM, 1: 43).

25. *Plato and Milton*, Cornell Studies in English, vol. 35 (Ithaca: Cornell University Press, 1947), pp. 5–9.

26. Reproduced in Harris F. Fletcher, *The Intellectual Development of John Milton* (Urbana: University of Illinois Press, 1956–61), 2: 637.

27. *An English Exposition of the Roman Antiquities* (London, 1623), p. 35 (*Early English Books, 1475–1640*, University Microfilm, Reel 1204).

28. Everyman ed. (London: J. M. Dent, 1907), 1: 160–61. For citations to Cudworth and Ralegh, see Bush, 1: 94–95.

29. The studies of Lily B. Campbell—"The Christian Muse," *Huntington Library Bulletin* 8 (October 1935), pp. 29–70, and *Divine Poetry and Drama in Sixteenth-Century England* (Berkeley and Los Angeles: University of California Press, 1959)—are relevant in documenting this point. On Christian rejection of the Muses, see Chap. 13, "The Muses," in Ernst Robert Curtius, *European Literature and the Latin Middle Ages*, trans. Willard R. Trask (New York: Harper and Row, 1953), esp. pp. 235–36 and 241.

30. Trans. Josuah Sylvester, *Bartas: His Devine Weekes and Workes* (1605; reprint ed., Gainesville: Scholars' Facsimiles & Reprints, 1965), pp. 540–41, st. 74, 78, 79.

31. Dedicatory Epistle to *The Spanish Friar* in *The Works of John Dryden*, ed. Sir Walter Scott and George Saintsbury (Edinburgh, 1883), 6: 407–408.

32. The line is "Immutable, Immortal, Infinite," Bk. 3, l.

373. Sylvester's influence on the youthful psalm paraphrases has often been noted, by Hanford and Tillyard, for example (Bush, 1: 112–13). William B. Hunter has seen the Sylvestrian influence on Milton's prosody as more sustained ("The Sources of Milton's Prosody," *Philological Quarterly* 28 [January 1949], 125–44). The story of Du Bartas's influence on English literature has been told many times, the most recent and balanced presentation of the subject being in Anne Lake Prescott, *French Poets and the English Renaissance* (New Haven: Yale University Press, 1978), Chap. 5, "Du Bartas." Some older work retains its utility. William Richardson Abbot, "Studies in the Influence of Du Bartas in England, 1584–1641," Ph.D. diss., University of North Carolina, 1931, exhaustively documents the extent of Du Bartas's popularity in England during the period covered by his dissertation. My own work, "Du Bartas and the Modes of Christian Poetry in England," Ph.D. diss., University of Oregon, 1965, surveys all the scholarship on Du Bartas's vogue and serves as a useful corrective to the older view that he was a prime influence on writers like Milton. That view was most notably expressed in George Coffin Taylor's *Milton's Use of Du Bartas* (Cambridge, Mass.: Harvard University Press, 1934).

33. *The Poetical Works of Edmund Spenser*, ed. J. C. Smith and Ernest de Selincourt (London: Oxford University Press, 1912), p. 485, ll. 512–20.

34. Milton to Gill, December 4, 1634 (CM, 12: 16–17). Hinting at a similar experience also is his description of Sonnet 7 as "some of my nightward thoughts some while since" in the two drafts of his "Letter to a Friend" (CM, 12: 322, 325).

35. Quoted in Arthur Koestler, *The Act of Creation* (New York: Macmillan, 1964), p. 117. Koestler brings together numerous examples of such experiences, drawn both from the sciences and the arts.

4. Long Choosing and Beginning Late

1. *Milton's Contemporary Reputation* (Columbus: Ohio State University Press, 1940), pp. 60–61, n. 4.

2. Sedulius and Paulinus are quoted in Curtius, *European*

Literature and the Latin Middle Ages, trans. Willard R. Trask (New York: Harper and Row, 1953), p. 235. For further discussion of Calliope/Clio, see Chap. 5.

3. Milton to Diodati, September [November?] 23, 1637 (CM, 12: 28).

4. *Reason of Church-Government* (CM, 3: 235–36).

5. *Poetical Works of Edmund Spenser,* ed. J. C. Smith and Ernest de Selincourt (London: Oxford University Press, 1912), p. 3. On the background of the *rota Vergilii,* see Curtius, *European Literature,* pp. 201n, 231–32.

6. For "De Poetica," see CM, 18: 139. See also Ruth Mohl's translation and notes in the *Complete Prose Works of John Milton,* ed. Don M. Wolfe (New Haven: Yale University Press, 1953), 1: 381–82. On the material in the Trinity MS, see CM, 18: 228–45. More useful, because it includes a usable facsimile of the Trinity MS itself, is the edition of John Milton, *Poems* (Menston, England: Scolar Press, 1972), pp. 35–42.

7. See the Scolar Press edition, pp. 4–5, for the poem's several drafts. The significance of these drafts for the composition of *Paradise Lost* was acutely analyzed by John Diekhoff in "The Trinity Manuscript and the Dictation of *Paradise Lost,*" *Philological Quarterly* 28 (January 1949), 52.

8. The anonymous biographer at least implies that Milton had been interested in the divorce question before his own problems occurred: "The lawfulness and expedience of this [divorce], duly regulat in order to all those purposes, for which Marriage was at first instituted; had upon full consideration & reading good Authors bin formerly his Opinion" (*Early Lives,* p. 23).

9. The best exposition of this remains Ernest Sirluck's "Milton's Idle Right Hand," *Journal of English and Germanic Philology* 60 (October 1961), 749–85.

10. Jonathan Richardson, *Explanatory Notes and Remarks on Milton's "Paradise Lost"* (*Early Lives,* p. 291).

11. *A Milton Handbook,* 4th ed. (New York: Appleton-Century-Crofts, 1946), p. 145.

12. The beginnings of the controversy lie in vol. 28 (January 1949) of *Philological Quarterly.* There Allan H. Gilbert argued "that the tragedy is essentially an early work, following

soon after the making of the notes in the Cambridge Manuscript" ("Is *Samson Agonistes* Unfinished?" p. 106). Far more influential were William Riley Parker's arguments for 1648–53, originally made in the same volume ("The Date of *Samson Agonistes,*" pp. 145–66) and subsequently repeated in his three other treatments of the subject: "The Date of *Samson Agonistes:* A Postscript," *Notes and Queries,* n.s. 5 (May 1958), 201–202; *Milton,* pp. 903–17; and "The Date of *Samson Agonistes* Again," in *Calm of Mind,* ed. Joseph Anthony Wittreich, Jr. (Cleveland: Case Western Reserve University Press, 1971), pp. 163–73. This last paper was a talk delivered Feb. 7, 1961, and prepared for the press by John T. Shawcross after Parker's death. It was Shawcross who provided the most cogent support for Parker in his metrical study of the three major poems: "The Chronology of Milton's Major Poems," *PMLA* 76 (September 1961), 345–58. The most penetrating attack on Parker was that of Sirluck, "Milton's Idle Right Hand," pp. 749–85, especially pp. 773–81; on Shawcross, that of Ants Oras in *Blank Verse and Chronology in Milton,* University of Florida Monographs in the Humanities, no. 20 (Gainesville: University Presses of Florida, 1966). Mary Ann Radzinowicz reviews the entire matter in *Toward "Samson Agonistes"* (Princeton: Princeton University Press, 1978), app. E, "The Date of Composition of *Samson Agonistes,*" pp. 387–407, and concludes: "Objective evidence is not lacking for the late date; artistic practices and theories do not militate against it; thematic links between *Paradise Lost* and *Samson Agonistes* confirm it; and the existence of allusions from autobiography and current affairs points so strongly to the late date that early daters have to expend heroic effort to discredit intentional and biographical readings in general before mounting their own claim that in *Samson Agonistes* Milton was anticipating in dread what late daters abundantly see him as already having undergone."

13. In his conversations with Aubrey, Phillips amended his "several years" to "about 15 or 16 yeares before ever his Poem was thought of" (*Early Lives,* p. 13).

14. Sirluck, whose above-cited essay so conclusively documents Milton's poetic drought, errs, I think, in his explanation for it, that the marriage violated previously made vows of celi-

bacy that Milton associated with his vocation as poet. Thus, its failure made him feel unfit to write poetry until blindness replaced chastity in his mind as the symbol of his calling: "He had offered God a sacrifice and then withdrawn it; he had pledged celibacy and then substituted marriage; had God rejected the substitute in anger? And if he had, was he also rejecting the service whose pledge had been withdrawn? . . . when at length he does regain his sense of inspiration its symbol will not be celibacy. . . . The new symbol of poetic inspiration will be his blindness" ("Milton's Idle Right Hand," pp. 770–71). Although Sirluck's complex arguments are well documented, they overlook such factors as Milton's association of celibacy and Popery and his life-long enthusiasm for feminine beauty.

15. As Paul H. Kocher has richly documented, the Elizabethans reconciled this view with their awareness of the regularity of nature "by emphasizing that God foresaw man's moral choices and so planned the order of nature from the first as to respond to them. So God foreknew what the sinfulness of the Elizabethans would be and arranged in advance for an earthquake in 1580, a plague in 1593, a flood in 1600, comets, droughts, storms, or crop failures in other years." Obviously, this doctrine extended to individuals as well: "His Providence extended to the smallest accidents of life and to the slightest needs of his human children. It was unthinkable that he would not use the forces of nature as agents of his anger or approval" (*Science and Religion in Elizabethan England* [San Marino: Huntington Library, 1953], pp. 94, 96).

16. *Life Records,* 3: 296–97. The *Life Records* contain many other expressions of this sentiment, those, for example, of Nicholas Heinsius (3: 252), John Heydon (4: 320), and John Taylor (4: 366).

17. John 9:1–7. As to whether the pool of Siloam is to be identified with Siloa's, disagreement among Miltonists exists. Those who feel that they should be identified include Jackson I. Cope, "Milton's Muse in *Paradise Lost,*" *Modern Philology* 55 (August 1957), 6–10, and sec. 1, "Muse and Poet in 'Paradise Lost,'" in Chap. 5, "The Creating Voice," (*The Metaphoric Structure of "Paradise Lost"* [Baltimore: Johns Hopkins Press,

1962], 149–64); Paul Lauter, "Milton's 'Siloa's Brook,'" *Notes and Queries,* n.s. 5 (May 1958), 204–205; Gerald Snare, "Milton's 'Siloa's Brook' Again," *Milton Quarterly* 4 (December 1970), 55–57; and Anthony Low, "Siloa's Brook: *Paradise Lost,* I, 11," *Milton Quarterly* 6 (October 1972), 3–5. Opponents include Ann Gossman and George W. Whiting, "Siloas Brook, the Pool of Siloam, and Milton's Muse," *Studies in Philology* 58 (January 1961), 193–205; and more recently, Leo Miller, "'Siloa's Brook' in *Paradise Lost:* Another View," *Milton Quarterly* 6 (October 1972), 5–7. Miller grants that "it is an inference easy to accept that Milton could have at any time associated 'Siloa brook' with 'Siloam pool.' That he thought a good deal about the episode of the blind man at Siloam pool (John 9) is equally plausible. What is still open to question is whether he necessarily always made the connection, particularly in the form 'Siloa'" (p. 6). His conclusion: "In the absence of direct evidence, that is a matter of exegetics, suitable indeed for a sermon, but as a matter of scholarly judgment, not proved" (p. 7). Such rigor is admirable in an age where critics all too often approach their texts as if they were so many Rorschach tests, but a certain bridging of the gaps is necessary for any critical reading to proceed. The real question becomes whether in terms of tradition and text alike, the bridge is defensible.

18. *The World of the Blind,* trans. Alys Hallard (New York: Macmillan, 1930), pp. 32–33.

19. "Critical Activity of the Poetic Mind: John Milton," *PMLA* 55 (September 1940), 772.

5. HEAV'NLY MUSE

1. "Three Muses and a Poet: A Perspective on Milton's Epic Thought," *Milton Studies* 10 (1977), 36.

2. For Hunter's arguments, see his "Milton's Muse" in *Bright Essence: Studies in Milton's Theology* by Hunter, C. A. Patrides, and J. H. Adamson (Salt Lake City: University of Utah Press, 1971), pp. 149–56; for Mollenkott's, see "Some Implications of Milton's Androgynous Muse," *Bucknell Review* 24 (Spring 1978), 27–36.

3. See, e.g., A. W. Verity's edition of Milton's *Paradise Lost* (Cambridge: Cambridge University Press, 1929), notes to 1: 1–16 (p. 368) and 1: 17–26 (p. 370). More recently, Dame Helen Gardner writes: "How are we to regard Milton's invocation of the Muse? Is she a metaphor for the Holy Spirit? Surely not; for he turns from his invocation of the Muse to a prayer to the Spirit, which is in quite a different tone" (*A Reading of "Paradise Lost"* [Oxford: Clarendon Press, 1965], pp. 18–19).

4. This is the punctuation as it appears in the MS in the Pierpont Morgan Library. See *The Manuscript of Milton's "Paradise Lost" Book I,* ed. Helen Darbishire (Oxford: Oxford University Press, 1931), for photographic facsimiles and comparison of MS with a copy of the first edition (pp. 2–3).

5. *Oxford Classical Dictionary,* 2d ed. (Oxford: Clarendon Press, 1972), s.v. "Muses."

6. Ll. 29–32 (CM, 1: 186–87).

7. Ll. 12–16 (CM, 1: 270–71).

8. Ll. 24–26 (CM, 1: 288–89).

9. *Variorum Commentary* 1: 84–85, 237–38, 241–42, 272. Since all further references are to vol. 1, only page numbers will be given subsequently.

10. On their ubiquity, see two notes of mine: "Spenser's Muse and the Dumaeus *Vergil*" (*Spenser Newsletter* 5 [Spring–Summer 1974], 10) and "More about Spenser and 'De Musarum Inventis,'" (*American Notes and Queries* 14 [January 1976], 67–71). The tag for Clio from the verses appears in the background of Plate 1. See n. 42 below.

11. Third ed. (London, 1559). An augmentation of Sir Thomas Elyot's *Dictionary* of 1538, Cooper's work both as *Bibliotheca Eliotae* and after 1565 as *Thesaurus Linguae Romanae et Britannicae* was very popular. According to Robert B. Gardiner it was in the school library at St. Paul's.

12. *The Minor Poems. The Works of Edmund Spenser: A Variorum Edition* (Baltimore: Johns Hopkins Press, 1943), 1: 43. All subsequent quotations of Spenser are to this edition, hereafter cited as *Var. Sp.*

13. Trans. Paul Shorey in *The Collected Dialogues of Plato,* ed.

Edith Hamilton and Huntington Cairns, Bollingen Series 71 (New York: Pantheon Books, 1961), p. 841.

14. Trans. William Harris Stahl, Records of Civilization, Sources and Studies, no. 48 (New York: Columbia University Press, 1952), p. 194.

15. William Harrison Woodward, ed., *Desiderius Erasmus concerning the Aim and Method of Education,* Classics in Education, no. 19 (1904; reprint ed., New York: Bureau of Publications, Teachers College, Columbia University, 1964), p. 167.

16. Minor Poems, *Var. Sp.,* 1: 244.

17. Eds. Karl K. Hulley and Stanley T. Vandersall (Lincoln: University of Nebraska Press, 1970), pp. 48, 248.

18. *A New Discovery of the Old Art of Teaching Schoole,* ed. E. T. Campagnac (Liverpool: The University Press, 1913), p. 162.

19. "Clio," *Notes and Queries,* n.s. 8 (May 1961), 178–79; *Complete English Poetry* (Garden City: Doubleday, 1963), p. 26; *Complete Poetry,* rev. ed. (Garden City: Doubleday, 1971), p. 46.

20. *Moralia,* trans. Frank Cole Babbitt, Loeb Classical Library (Cambridge, Mass.: Harvard University Press, 1936), 5: 302–303.

21. *The Poems of John Milton,* ed. John Carey and Alastair Fowler (Longman ed., 1968; reprint ed. New York: W. W. Norton, 1972), pp. 55–56, 149.

22. "Amiot to the Readers," *The Lives of the Noble Grecians and Romanes,* trans. Thomas North (Stratford-upon-Avon: Shakespeare Head Press, 1928), 1: xiv.

23. *The Poetical Works of John Milton* (London: Macmillan, 1882), 3: 313.

24. *The Latin Poems of John Milton,* Cornell Studies in English, no. 15 (New Haven: Yale University Press, 1930), pp. 307–308.

25. "Notes on Milton's Early Development," *University of Toronto Quarterly* 13 (October 1943), 90.

26. *Paradise Regained, The Minor Poems, and Samson Agonistes* (New York: Odyssey, 1937), p. 274.

27. *Complete Poems and Major Prose* (New York: Odyssey, 1957), p. 83.

28. (Basel, 1584). The translations that follow are my own.

29. (Paris, 1553).
30. *Thesaurus Linguae Latinae*, 4 vols. in 2 (Lyons, 1573).
31. Translated from the fac. ed. (New York, Hildesheim: George Olms, 1970), p. 346. The reference to Cornutus is to the following sentences in *De Natura Deorum:* "Caeterum Clio una e numero Musarum est, ἀπὸ τοῦ κλέους, id est a gloria sic dicta. Et quare? Quod docti gloriam consequantur, & etiam alios gloria illustrare possint" (Basel, 1543), p. 18 ("For the rest, Clio is one from the number of the Muses, *apo tou kleous*, that is so called from glory. And why? Because the learned pursue glory and also are able to make others illustrious with glory").
32. *History of Britain* (CM, 10: 32).
33. *The First Defence* (CM, 7: 9).
34. *Fulgentius the Mythographer*, trans. Leslie George Whitbread (Columbus: Ohio State University Press, 1971), pp. 55–56.
35. (Basel, 1570), p. 125.
36. *Opera omnia* (Leyden, 1696), 2: 563.
37. *Complete English Poetry*, p. 26; *Complete Poetry*, rev. ed., p. 46.
38. *Reason of Church-Government* (CM, 3: 236).
39. Frederick Morgan Padelford, trans., *Select Translations from Scaliger's Poetics*, Yale Studies in English, no. 26 (New York: Henry Holt, 1905), p. 54 (bk. 3, chap. 96).
40. *The Enduring Monument* (Chapel Hill: University of North Carolina Press, 1962).
41. (London, 1678), s.v. "Clio." I document the Spenserians' quarrel and give other evidence for Clio as Spenser's muse in the brief articles cited in n. 10 above.
42. Figures 1 and 2 appear in Raimond van Marle's *Iconographie de l'art profane au moyen age et à la renaissance*, vol. II, *Allégories et symboles* (The Hague: Martinus Nijhoff, 1932), pp. 270, fig. 300, and 267, fig. 297. Guy de Tervarent also discusses the swan as an attribute of Clio in *Attributs et Symboles dans l'Art Profane, 1450–1600: Dictionnaire d'un Langage Perdu*, 2 vols. in 1 (Geneva: Librairie E. Droz, 1958), 1, col. 139.
43. See Figure 3, from a copy in the Lewis Collection, Texas Christian University Library.

44. Edgar Wind, *Pagan Mysteries of the Renaissance* (London: Faber and Faber, 1958), p. 113. The frontispiece is reproduced on p. 47. For an example of the averted Urania that Wind cites (p. 114, n. 1), see Figure 4, the title page of Hyginus' *Astronomi de Mundi et Sphere* (Venice, 1502), from a copy in the Department of Rare Books and Special Collections, University of Michigan, Ann Arbor. The opposed figure, though labeled Astronomia, suggests Clio with her down-turned eyes and open book. The paired figures were themselves the visual commonplace. Though often labeled as Clio and Urania, they were sometimes identified differently.

45. Wind, p. 127. *Pagan Mysteries* also includes a reproduction of this engraving (fig. 38). I reproduce it here (Figure 5) through the courtesy of a private collection.

46. *Book of the Courtier*, trans. Sir Thomas Hoby, Everyman ed. (London: J. M. Dent, 1928), p. 276; *The Boke named the Gouernour*, Everyman ed. (London: J. M. Dent, 1907), p. 104.

47. *Of the Citie of God*, trans. J. H. (n.p., 1610), p. 225.

48. *Odes and Epodes*, bk. 3, ode 30, Loeb Classical Library, trans. C. E. Bennett (Cambridge, Mass.: Harvard University Press, 1927), p. 279.

49. Lines 47–51, Temple Classics (London: J. M. Dent, 1932), p. 265.

50. Lines 91–102, Temple Classics (London: J. M. Dent, 1933), p. 133.

51. *Milton and the Renaissance Hero* (Oxford: Clarendon Press, 1967), p. 1.

52. *Bright Essence* (Salt Lake City: University of Utah Press, 1971), p. 153.

53. Pages 231–33. The dozens of references to God as Maker that Ernst Robert Curtius cites are highly relevant to our understanding of this image. *European Literature and the Latin Middle Ages*, trans. Willard R. Trask (New York: Harper and Row, 1953), pp. 544–46.

54. "The Christian Muse," pp. 45, 69.

55. *Moralia*, 5: 302–303.

56. Trans. Sir John Harington, ed. Robert McNulty (Oxford: Clarendon Press, 1972), p. 19.

57. In his *Classical Mythology in Literature, Art, and Music*,

Philip Mayerson notes that Polyhymnia and Clio were also sometimes named as Orpheus's mother (Waltham, Mass., Toronto: Xerox, 1971), p. 270.

6. IN HIS BLINDNESS SEEING ALL

1. On Santayana's remark, see Noel Stock, *The Life of Ezra Pound* (New York: Pantheon Books, 1970), p. 374. See also *The Paideia Proposal* (New York: Macmillan, 1982).

2. "Advice to Youth," with Allen Ginsberg in *Allen Verbatim: Lectures on Poetry, Politics, Consciousness,* ed. Gordon Ball (New York: McGraw-Hill, 1974), pp. 105–106.

3. *Allen Verbatim,* p. 110. That some of the authors Duncan studied in the classroom became his masters is evidenced by his lifelong reverence for Robert Browning, alluded to above and more fully spelled out in his essay, "Man's Fulfillment in Order and Strife," *Fictive Certainties* (New York: New Directions, 1985), pp. 112–13.

4. *Life Records,* 5: 47.

5. *The Life of Adam Martindale, Written by Himself,* ed. Richard Parkinson, Chetham Society Publications 4 (Manchester: Charles Simms, 1845), p. 15. I place Martindale's comments in context in chap. 2 above.

6. Milton to Emeric Bigot, March 24, 1656 (CM, 12: 85–87), quoted in chap. 1 above.

7. "Tradition and the Individual Talent," *Selected Essays* (New York: Harcourt, Brace & World, 1960), p. 10.

8. "Personal Mood Transmuted into Epic: T. S. Eliot's *Waste Land,*" in *The American Quest for a Supreme Fiction* (Chicago and London: University of Chicago Press, 1979), pp. 101–25.

9. *Biographia Literaria,* ed. John Shawcross (Oxford: Clarendon Press, 1907), p. 5.

10. For Byron, see *Don Juan: A Variorum Edition,* ed. Truman Guy Steffan and Willis W. Pratt (Austin: University of Texas Press, 1957), 2: 274, III, i, 1. For Robinson, see his *Collected Poems* (New York: Macmillan, 1937), p. 93.

Notes to Chapter 6

11. (Boston: Little, Brown, 1982), p. 118.

12. *The Anxiety of Influence: A Theory of Poetry* (New York: Oxford University Press, 1973), p. 33. Some of these studies I list in chap. 1.

13. Richard J. DuRocher, *Milton and Ovid* (Ithaca and London: Cornell University Press, 1985); Mary Campbell Brill, "Milton and Ovid," Ph.D. diss., Cornell University, 1935.

BIBLIOGRAPHY

Abbot, William Richardson. "Studies in the Influence of Du-Bartas in England, 1584–1641." Ph.D. dissertation, University of North Carolina, 1931.
Ariosto, Lodovico. *Orlando Furioso*. Translated by Sir John Harington. Edited by Robert McNulty. Oxford: Clarendon Press, 1972.
Augustine, Saint. *Of the Citie of God*. Translated by J. H. 1610.
———. *On Christian Doctrine*. Translated by D. W. Robertson. Library of Liberal Arts. Indianapolis: Bobbs-Merrill, 1958.
Ausonius. Translated by Hugh G. Evelyn-White. 2 vols. Loeb Classical Library. Cambridge, Mass.: Harvard University Press, 1919. Reprint 1961.
Baldwin, Ruth M. "Alexander Gill, the Elder, High Master of St. Paul's School: An Approach to Milton's Intellectual Development." Ph.D. dissertation, University of Illinois, 1955.
Baldwin, T. W. *William Shakspere's Petty School*. Urbana: University of Illinois Press, 1943.
———. *William Shakspere's Small Latine & Lesse Greeke*. 2 vols. Urbana: University of Illinois Press, 1944.
Barker, Arthur. "Milton's Schoolmasters." *Modern Language Review* 32 (October 1937): 517–36.
Bloom, Harold. *The Anxiety of Influence: A Theory of Poetry*. New York: Oxford University Press, 1973.
Brennecke, Ernest, Jr. *John Milton the Elder and His Music*. Co-

lumbia University Studies in Musicology, no. 2. New York: Columbia University Press, 1938.

Brill, Mary Campbell. "Milton and Ovid." Ph.D. dissertation, Cornell University, 1935.

Brinsley, John. *Ludus Literarius.* Edited by E.T. Campagnac. Liverpool: The University Press, 1917.

Buchler, Joannes. *Sacrarum Profanarumque Phraseum Poeticarum Thesaurus.* London: 1632. University Microfilm, *Early English Books, 1475–1640,* reel 1299. Ann Arbor, Michigan.

Bush, Douglas. *A Variorum Commentary on the Poems of John Milton,* Vol. 1, *The Latin and Greek Poems.* New York: Columbia University Press, 1970.

──────, and A. S. P. Woodhouse. *A Variorum Commentary on the Poems of John Milton,* Vol. 2, *The Minor English Poems.* New York: Columbia University Press, 1972.

Byron, George Gordon, Lord. *Don Juan: A Variorum Edition.* Edited by Truman Guy Steffan and Willis W. Pratt. Austin: University of Texas Press, 1957.

Calepinus, Ambrosius. *Dictionarium Octo Linguarum.* Basel: 1584.

Campbell, Lily B. "The Christian Muse." *Huntington Library Bulletin* 8 (October 1935): 29–70.

──────. *Divine Poetry and Drama in Sixteenth-Century England.* Berkeley and Los Angeles: University of California Press, 1959.

Castiglione, Baldesar. *Book of the Courtier.* Translated by Sir Thomas Hoby. Everyman Edition. London: J. M. Dent, 1928.

Charlton, Kenneth. "The Educational Background." In *The Age of Milton.* Edited by C. A. Patrides and Raymond B. Waddington, pp. 102–37. Manchester: Manchester University Press, 1980.

Chifos, Eugenia. "Alexander Gill the Younger's Relationship with John Milton." Master's thesis, Ohio State University, 1945.

──────. "Milton's Letter to Gill, May 20, 1628." *MLN* 62 (January 1947): 37–39.

Cicero. *The Letters to His Friends.* Translated by W. Glynn Williams. 3 vols. Loeb Classical Library. Cambridge,

Mass.: Harvard University Press, 1927.

———. *Tusculan Disputations*. Translated by J. E. King. Loeb Classical Library. Cambridge, Mass.: Harvard University Press, 1945.

Clark, Donald Lemen. "John Milton and William Chappell." *Huntington Library Quarterly* 18 (August 1955): 329–50.

———. *John Milton at St. Paul's School*. New York: Columbia University Press, 1948. Reprint, Archon Books, 1964.

Coleridge, Samuel T. *Biographia Literaria*. Edited by John Shawcross. Oxford: Clarendon Press, 1907.

Cooper, Thomas. *Bibliotheca Eliotae*. 3d tyme corrected. London: 1559.

Cope, Jackson I. *The Metaphoric Structure of "Paradise Lost."* Baltimore: Johns Hopkins Press, 1962.

———. "Milton's Muse in *Paradise Lost*." *Modern Philology* 55 (August 1957): 6–10.

Cornutus. *De Natura Deorum*. Basel: 1543.

Costello, William T., S.J. *The Scholastic Curriculum at Early Seventeenth-Century Cambridge*. Cambridge, Mass.: Harvard University Press, 1958.

Curtius, Ernst Robert. *European Literature and the Latin Middle Ages*. Translated by Willard R. Trask. New York: Harper and Row, 1953.

———. "The Muses." *Zeitschrift für Romanisch Philologie* 59 (1939): 129–88; 63 (1943): 256–68.

Dante. *Inferno*. Temple Classics. London: J. M. Dent, 1932.

———. *Purgatorio*. Temple Classics. London: J. M. Dent, 1933.

Darbishire, Helen, ed. *The Early Lives of Milton*. London: Constable, 1932.

———, ed. *The Manuscript of Milton's "Paradise Lost" Book I*. Oxford: Oxford University Press, 1931.

Davies, Godfrey. *The Early Stuarts*. 2d ed. London: Oxford University Press for Readers Union, 1964.

Dessner, Lawrence Jay. *How to Write a Poem*. New York: Washington Mews Books, 1979.

Diekhoff, John. "Critical Activity of the Poetic Mind: John Milton." *PMLA* 55 (September 1940): 748–72.

———. "The Trinity Manuscript and the Dictation of *Paradise*

Lost." *Philological Quarterly* 28 (January 1949): 44–52.
Dryden, John. *The Works.* Edited by Sir Walter Scott and George Saintsbury, vol. 6. Edinburgh: W. Paterson, 1883.
Du Bartas, Guillaume de Salluste, Sieur. *Bartas: His Devine Weekes and Workes.* Translated by Josuah Sylvester. 1605. Reprint. Gainesville: Scholars' Facsimiles and Reprints, 1965.
Duncan, Robert. *Fictive Certainties.* New York: New Directions, 1985.
DuRocher, Richard J. *Milton and Ovid.* Ithaca: Cornell University Press, 1985.
Eliot, T. S. *Selected Essays.* New York: Harcourt, Brace & World, 1960.
Elyot, Sir Thomas. *The Boke named the Gouernour.* Everyman Edition. London: J. M. Dent, 1907.
Erasmus, Desiderius. *Desiderius Erasmus concerning the Aim and Method of Education.* Edited by William Harrison Woodward. 1904. Classics in Education, No. 19. Reprint. New York: Bureau of Publications, Teachers College, Columbia University, 1964.
―――. *Le Banquet Poétique.* Edited by Verdun L. Saulnier. Melun: Librairie D'Argences, 1948.
Fink, Zera S. "Wine, Poetry, and Milton's Elegia Sexta." *English Studies* 21 (1939): 164–65.
Fletcher, Harris F. *The Intellectual Development of John Milton.* 2 vols. Vol. 1, *The Institution to 1625: From the Beginnings through Grammar School* (1956); Vol. 2, *The Cambridge University Period, 1625–1632* (1961). Urbana: University of Illinois Press.
Fowles, John. *Mantissa.* Boston: Little, Brown, 1982.
Freeman, James A., and Anthony Low, guest eds. *Urbane Milton: The Latin Poetry. Milton Studies* 19 (1984).
French, J. Milton. *Life Records of John Milton.* 5 vols. Rutgers University Studies in English, no. 7. New Brunswick: Rutgers University Press, 1949–58.
Fulgentius the Mythographer. Translated by Leslie George Whitbread. Columbus: Ohio State University Press, 1971.
Gardiner, Robert B. *The Admission Registers of St. Paul's School.* London: George Bell, 1884.

Gardner, Helen. *A Reading of "Paradise Lost."* Oxford: Clarendon Press, 1965.
Gilbert, Allan H. "Is *Samson Agonistes* Unfinished?" *Philological Quarterly* 28 (January 1949): 98–106.
Ginsberg, Allen. *Allen Verbatim: Lectures on Poetry, Politics, Consciousness.* Edited by Gordon Ball. New York: McGraw-Hill, 1974.
―――. *Collected Poems, 1947–1980.* New York: Harper and Row, 1984.
Godwin, Thomas. *An English Exposition of the Roman Antiquities.* London: 1623. University Microfilm, *Early English Books, 1475–1640,* Reel 1204. Ann Arbor, Michigan.
Greene, Thomas M. *The Light in Troy: Imitation and Discovery in Renaissance Poetry.* New Haven: Yale University Press, 1982.
Gregory, E. R. "Du Bartas and the Modes of Christian Poetry in England." Ph.D. dissertation, University of Oregon, 1965.
―――. "More about Spenser and 'De Musarum Inventis.'" *American Notes and Queries* 14 (January 1976): 67–71.
―――. "Spenser's Muse and the Dumaeus *Vergil.*" *Spenser Newsletter,* no. 5 (Spring–Summer 1974): 10.
―――. "Three Muses and a Poet: A Perspective on Milton's Epic Thought." *Milton Studies* 10 (1977): 35–64.
Guillory, John. *Poetic Authority: Spenser, Milton, and Literary History.* New York: Columbia University Press, 1983.
Gyraldus, Lilius Gregorius. *De Musis Syntagma,* in *Opera Omnia.* Leyden: 1696.
Hammond, N. G. L., and H. H. Scullard, eds. *Oxford Classical Dictionary.* 2d ed. Oxford: Clarendon Press, 1970.
Hanford, James Holly. *John Milton: Englishman.* New York: Crown, 1949.
―――. *A Milton Handbook.* 4th ed. New York: Appleton-Century-Crofts, 1946.
Harding, Davis P. *Milton and the Renaissance Ovid.* Illinois Studies in Language and Literature, 30, no. 4. Urbana: University of Illinois Press, 1946.
Hardison, O. B., Jr. *The Enduring Monument: A Study of the Idea of Praise in Renaissance Literary Theory and Practice.* Chapel

Hill: University of North Carolina Press, 1962.
Hazlitt, William. *The Complete Works.* Vol. 5. London: J. M. Dent, 1930.
Henry, Nathaniel. "The Mystery of Milton's Muse." *Renaissance Papers* 12 (1967): 69–83.
Hesiod. *The Poems.* Translated by R. M. Frazer. Norman: University of Oklahoma Press, 1983.
Hill, Christopher. *Milton and the English Revolution.* London: Faber and Faber, 1977.
Hobbes, Thomas. *The English Works.* Edited by Sir William Molesworth. 1840. Reprint, Darmstadt: Scientia Verlag Aalen, 1966.
Hooker, Richard. *Laws of Ecclesiastical Polity.* Everyman Edition. London: J. M. Dent, 1907.
Hoole, Charles. *A New Discovery of the Old Art of Teaching Schoole.* Edited by E. T. Campagnac. Liverpool: The University Press, 1913.
Horace. *Odes and Epodes.* Translated by C. E. Bennett. Loeb Classical Library. Cambridge, Mass.: Harvard University Press, 1927.
Hunter, William B., Jr. "Milton's Muse." In *Bright Essence: Studies in Milton's Theology,* pp. 149–56. Salt Lake City: University of Utah Press, 1971.
―――. "Milton's Urania." *Studies in English Literature* 4 (Winter 1964): 35–42.
―――. "The Sources of Milton's Prosody." *Philological Quarterly* 28 (January 1949): 125–44.
Hyginus, C. Iulius. *Astronomi de Mundi et Sphere.* Venice: 1502.
―――. *Fabularum Liber.* Basel: 1570.
Jaynes, Julian. *The Origin of Consciousness in the Breakdown of the Bicameral Mind.* Boston: Houghton Mifflin, 1976.
Jonson, Ben. *Complete Poetry.* Edited by William B. Hunter, Jr. Garden City: Doubleday, 1963.
Juvenal. *Juvenal and Persius.* Translated by G. G. Ramsay. Loeb Classical Library. Cambridge, Mass.: Harvard University Press, 1940.
Kerrigan, William. *The Sacred Complex: On the Psychogenesis of Paradise Lost.* Cambridge, Mass.: Harvard University Press, 1983.

Kocher, Paul H. *Science and Religion in Elizabethan England*. San Marino: Huntington Library, 1953.
Koestler, Arthur. *The Act of Creation*. New York: Macmillan, 1964.
Langdon, Ida. *Milton's Theory of Poetry and Fine Art*. Cornell Studies in English. New Haven: Yale University Press, 1924.
Lauter, Paul. "Milton's 'Siloa's Brook.'" *Notes and Queries*, n.s. 5 (May 1958): 204–205.
Leach, A. F. "Milton as Schoolboy and Schoolmaster." *Proceedings of the British Academy* 3 (1907–08): 295–318.
Lewis, Charlton T., and Charles Short, eds. *A Latin Dictionary*. Oxford: Clarendon Press, 1879.
Lily, William. *A Shorte Introduction of Grammar*. Edited by Vincent J. Flynn. New York: Scholars' Facsimiles and Reprints, 1945.

———. *A Short Introduction of Grammar, 1549*. Menston, England: Scolar Press, 1970.
Little, Marguerite. "Milton's Ad Patrem and the Younger Gill's In Natalem Mei Parentis." *Journal of English and Germanic Philology* 49 (July 1950): 345–51.
Littleton, Adam. *A Latine dictionary*. London, 1678.
Livy. *From the Founding of the City*, vol. 1. Translated by B. O. Foster. 14 vols. Loeb Classical Library. Cambridge, Mass.: Harvard University Press, 1919.
Low, Anthony. "Siloa's Brook: *Paradise Lost*, I, 11." *Milton Quarterly* 6 (October 1972): 3–5.

———. "The Unity of Milton's *Elegia Sexta*." *English Literary Renaissance* 11 (Spring 1981): 213–23.
Macrobius. *Commentary on the Dream of Scipio*. Translated by William Harris Stahl. Records of Civilization, Sources and Studies, no. 48. New York: Columbia University Press, 1952.
Marle, Raimond van. *Iconographie de l'art profane au moyen age et à la renaissance*. The Hague: Martinus Nijhoff, 1932.
Martindale, Adam. *The Life of Adam Martindale, Written by Himself*. Edited by Richard Parkinson. Chetham Society Publications, vol. 4. Manchester: Charles Simms, 1845.
Mayerson, Philip. *Classical Mythology in Literature, Art, and Mu-*

sic. Waltham, Mass., Toronto: Xerox Publishing Co., 1971.

Miller, James E., Jr. *The American Quest for a Supreme Fiction.* Chicago: University of Chicago Press, 1979.

Miller, Leo. "'Siloa's Brook' in *Paradise Lost:* Another View." *Milton Quarterly* 6 (October 1972): 5–7.

Milton, John. *Complete English Poetry.* Edited by John T. Shawcross. Garden City: Doubleday, 1963.

———. *Complete Poems and Major Prose.* Edited by Merritt Y. Hughes. New York: Odyssey, 1957.

———. *Complete Poetry.* Rev. ed. Edited by John T. Shawcross. Garden City: Doubleday, 1971.

———. *Complete Prose Works.* Edited by Don M. Wolfe, vol. 1. New Haven: Yale University Press, 1953.

———. *The Latin Poems.* Edited by Walter MacKellar. Cornell Studies in English, no. 15. New Haven: Yale University Press, 1930.

———. *Paradise Lost.* Edited by A. W. Verity. Cambridge: Cambridge University Press, 1929.

———. *Paradise Regained, the Minor Poems, and Samson Agonistes.* Edited by Merritt Y. Hughes. New York: Odyssey, 1937.

———. *The Poems.* Edited by John Carey and Alastair Fowler. Longman edition, 1968. Reprint, New York: W. W. Norton, 1972.

———. *Poems Reproduced in Facsimile from the Manuscript in Trinity College, Cambridge.* Menston, England: Scolar Press, 1972.

———. *Poetical Works.* Edited by David Masson. 3 vols. London: Macmillan, 1882.

———. *The Works.* Edited by Frank Allen Patterson et al. New York: Columbia University Press, 1931–38.

Mollenkott, Virginia R. "Some Implications of Milton's Androgynous Muse." *Bucknell Review* 24 (Spring 1978): 27–36.

Oras, Ants. *Blank Verse and Chronology in Milton.* University of Florida Monographs in the Humanities, no. 20. Gainesville: University Presses of Florida, 1966.

Ovid. *Metamorphosis: Englished, Mythologized and Represented in*

Bibliography

Figures by George Sandys. Edited by Karl K. Hulley and Stanley T. Vandersall. Lincoln: University of Nebraska Press, 1970.

———. *Tristia*. Translated by Arthur Leslie Wheeler. Loeb Classical Library. Cambridge, Mass.: Harvard University Press, 1965.

Paideia Group. *The Paideia Proposal*. New York: Macmillan, 1982.

Parker, William Riley. "The Date of *Samson Agonistes*." *Philological Quarterly* 28 (January 1949): 145–66.

———. "The Date of *Samson Agonistes:* A Postscript." *Notes and Queries*, n.s. 5 (May 1958): 201–202.

———. "The Date of *Samson Agonistes* Again." In *Calm of Mind*. Edited by Joseph Anthony Wittreich, Jr., pp. 163–73. Cleveland: The Press of Case Western Reserve University, 1971.

———. *Milton: A Biography*. 2 vols. Oxford: Clarendon Press, 1968.

———. *Milton's Contemporary Reputation*. Columbus: Ohio State University Press, 1940.

———. Review of E. M. W. Tillyard, *The Miltonic Setting*. In *MLN* 55 (March 1940): 215–18.

Pigman, G. W. III. "Versions of Imitation in the Renaissance." *Renaissance Quarterly* 33 (Spring 1980): 1–32.

Platner, Samuel Ball, and Thomas Ashby, eds. *A Topographical Dictionary of Ancient Rome*. Oxford: Oxford University Press, 1929.

Plato. *Collected Dialogues*. Edited by Edith Hamilton and Huntington Cairns. Bollingen Series 71. New York: Pantheon Books, 1961.

Plutarch. *The Lives of the Noble Grecians and Romanes*. Translated by Thomas North. Stratford-upon-Avon: Shakespeare Head Press, 1928.

———. *Plutarch's Lives*. Translated by Bernadotte Perrin. 11 vols. Loeb Classical Library. Cambridge, Mass.: Harvard University Press, 1914.

———. *Moralia*. Translated by Frank Cole Babbitt. 15 vols. Loeb Classical Library. Cambridge, Mass.: Harvard University Press, 1936.

Prescott, Anne Lake. *French Poets and the English Renaissance.* New Haven: Yale University Press, 1978.
Quilligan, Maureen. *Milton's Spenser: The Politics of Reading.* Ithaca: Cornell University Press, 1983.
Quintilian. *Institutio Oratoria.* In *Ancient Literary Criticism.* Edited by D. A. Russell and Michael Winterbottom, pp. 372–423. Oxford: Clarendon Press, 1972.
Radzinowicz, Mary Ann. *Toward "Samson Agonistes": The Growth of Milton's Mind.* Princeton: Princeton University Press, 1978.
Rapaport, Herman. *Milton and the Postmodern.* Lincoln and London: University of Nebraska Press, 1983.
Ripa, Cesare. *Iconologia.* Fac. ed. New York, Hildesheim: George Olms, 1970.
Robins, Harry F. *If This Be Heresy: A Study of Milton and Origen.* Illinois Studies in Language and Literature, no. 51. Urbana: University of Illinois Press, 1963.
Robinson, Edwin Arlington. *Collected Poems.* New York: Macmillan, 1937.
Ross, Alexander. *Mystagogus Poeticus* or *The Muses Interpreter.* 2d ed. London: Richard Whitaker, 1648.
Samuel, Irene. *Plato and Milton.* Cornell Studies in English, vol. 35. Ithaca: Cornell University Press, 1947.
Scaliger, Julius Caesar. *Select Translations from Scaliger's Poetics.* Translated by Frederick Morgan Padelford. Yale Studies in English, no. 26. New York: Henry Holt, 1905.
Shaheen, Naseeb. "Milton's Muse and the *De Doctrina.*" *Milton Quarterly* 3 (October 1974): 72–76.
Shawcross, John T. "The Chronology of Milton's Major Poems." *PMLA* 76 (September 1961): 345–58.
———. "Clio." *Notes and Queries,* n.s. 8 (May 1961): 178–80.
Sirluck, Ernest. "Milton's Idle Right Hand." *Journal of English and Germanic Philology* 60 (October 1961): 749–85.
Snare, Gerald. "Milton's 'Siloa's Brook' Again." *Milton Quarterly* 4 (December 1970): 55–57.
Spenser, Edmund. *The Minor Poems. The Works of Edmund Spenser: A Variorum Edition.* Edited by Charles Grosvenor Osgood and Henry Gibbons Lotspeich. Baltimore: Johns Hopkins Press, 1943.

―――. *Poetical Works.* Edited by J. C. Smith and Ernest de Selincourt. London: Oxford University Press, 1912.
Steadman, John M. *Milton and the Renaissance Hero.* Oxford: Clarendon Press, 1967.
Stephanus, Carolus. *Dictionarium Historicum ac Poeticum.* Paris: 1553.
Stephanus, Robertus. *Thesaurus Linguae Latinae.* Lyons: 1573.
Stevens, Paul. *Imagination and the Presence of Shakespeare in Paradise Lost.* Madison: University of Wisconsin Press, 1985.
Stock, Noel. *The Life of Ezra Pound.* New York: Pantheon, 1970.
Taylor, George Coffin. *Milton's Use of Du Bartas.* Cambridge, Mass.: Harvard University Press, 1934.
Tervarent, Guy de. *Attributs et Symboles dans l'Art Profane, 1450–1600: Dictionnaire d'un Langage Perdu.* 2 vols. in 1. Geneva: Librairie E. Droz, 1958.
Tillyard, E. M. W. *The Miltonic Setting.* London: Chatto and Windus, 1938.
Turner, W. Arthur. "The Known English Acquaintances of John Milton." Ph.D. dissertation, Ohio State University, 1947.
Tuve, Rosemond. *Images and Themes in Five Poems by Milton.* Cambridge, Mass.: Harvard University Press, 1957.
Varro. *On the Latin Language.* Translated by Roland G. Kent. 2 vols. Loeb Classical Library. Cambridge, Mass.: Harvard University Press, 1951.
Virgil. *Virgil with an English Translation.* Translated by H. Rushton Fairclough. 2 vols. Rev. ed. Loeb Classical Library. Cambridge, Mass.: Harvard University Press, 1934.
Villey, Pierre. *The World of the Blind.* Translated by Alys Hallard. New York: Macmillan, 1930.
Vitruvius. *On Architecture.* Translated by Frank Granger. 2 vols. Loeb Classical Library. Cambridge, Mass.: Harvard University Press, 1934.
Wallerstein, Ruth. *Studies in Seventeenth-Century Poetic.* Madison: University of Wisconsin Press, 1950.
Warmington, E. H., trans. *Remains of Old Latin.* Loeb Classical Library. Cambridge, Mass.: Harvard University Press, 1936.
Watson, Foster. *The English Grammar Schools to 1660.* 1908.

Bibliography

Reprint. New York: Augustus M. Kelley, 1970.
Webber, Joan. "Walking on Water: Milton, Stevens, and Contemporary Poetry." In *Milton and the Line of Vision*. Edited by Joseph Anthony Wittreich, Jr., pp. 231–68. Madison: University of Wisconsin Press, 1975.
Whiting, George W., and Ann Gossman. "Siloas Brook, the Pool of Siloam, and Milton's Muse." *Studies in Philology* 58 (January 1961): 193–205.
Wind, Edgar. *Pagan Mysteries of the Renaissance*. London: Faber and Faber, 1958.
Wittreich, Joseph Anthony, Jr. *Visionary Poetics: Milton's Tradition and His Legacy*. San Marino: Huntington Library, 1979.
Woodhouse, A. S. P. "Notes on Milton's Early Development." *University of Toronto Quarterly* 13 (October 1943): 66–101.

INDEX

Amyot, Jacques: definition of history, 102
Anacreon, 49
Ariosto, Ludovico, 122
Aristotle, 39
Arthur, King, 112
Aubrey, John, 28, 61; *Brief Lives*, 16
Augustine, St., 3; contempt for glory, 117

Bacon, Sir Francis, 49
Baldwin, T. W.: on grammar school curriculum, 40
Birch, Thomas, 91
Blake, William, 127
Blindness, 74, 84; inward vision and, 85, 87, 88; as divine punishment, 86, 87; source of strength, 86; as sacrifice, 87
Bloom, Harold, 132
Boccaccio: *De Genealogiae Deorum gentilium*, 106
Borges, Jorge Luis, 130
Bridgewater MS, 89
Brill, Mary Campbell: Milton and Ovid, 132
Brinsley, John: *Ludus Literarius*, 24; on language study, 29, 30; "Grammatical translation," 29–30; on poetic composition, 30

Browning, Robert, 127
Buchler, Joannes, 50; *Sacrarum Profanarumque Phraseum Poeticarum Thesaurus*, 31–32
Bush, Douglas, 60, 61, 97, 99, 102
Byron, George Gordon, Lord: "Hail, Muse! *et cetera*," 130

Cadmon: divine inspiration, 82
Calchas, 58
Calepinus, Ambrosius: *Dictionarium Octo Linguarum*, 104; Clio and glory, 104
Calliope. *See* Muses
Cambridge, 40, 41, 42; curriculum, 35. *See also* University
Camenae, 46, 50; in Buchler, 31; origin, 51; associations, 53, 54, 57; Numa, 54; characteristics, 56; etymology, 56; genealogy, 56; inspiration by, 58; interchangeable with muses, 59. *See also* Muses
Campbell, Lily B., 121
Carey, John, 102
Castiglione, Baldasare, 117
Cato: *Disticha Moralia*, 19
Chaucer, Geoffrey, 127
Christianity: muses and, 11, 12; pagan tradition, 66

Index

Cicero, 11, 18, 20, 40, 57, 128; muses, 3, 42; *Epistles*, 35, 36, 40–41; *musae mansuetiores*, 37, 39, 42; Epistle to Lentulus, 39; Milton's first prolusion and, 42, 43
Clark, Donald Lemen, 41
Clarke, John: *Quaestiones aliquot declamatoriae*, 37, 47–48
Clio. *See* Muses
Coleridge, Samuel Taylor, 129
Comes, Natalis, 48–49, 99, 101; *Mythologiae*, 100
Cooper, Thomas: *Bibliotheca Eliotae*, 23, 34, 99; also listed as *Thesaurus*, 28, 41, 99; muses, 42, 59
Cope, Jackson I.: Siloam/Siloa's Brook, 148
Cornutus: quoted in Ripa, 105, 152; Clio and glory, 152 (n. 31)
Creativity, 45, 71, 82, 145 (n. 35)
Cudworth, Ralph, 66

Dante: *Inferno*, 117; *Purgatorio*, 118; condemns worldly glory, 118
Darbishire, Helen: *Paradise Lost* manuscript, 150 (n. 4)
Davenant, William: Hobbes's defense of, 12
Dell, William: rejection of muses, 11
Dessner, Lawrence Jay: *How to Write a Poem*, 5–6
Diekhoff, John, 90; composition of *Paradise Lost*, 146 (n. 7)
Diodati, Charles, 47, 50, 53, 59, 61, 75, 117; Milton's correspondence with, 15; Milton's "Elegy 6" and, 46; disposition, 15, 47
Dryden, John: on Josuah Sylvester, 68; Milton's kinship with Spenser, 128
Du Bartas, Guillaume de Salluste, Sieur, 4, 69, 72, 119, 120, 124; *L'Uranie*, 67–68; Christian poetry, 67–68; influence, 145 (n. 32)
Duncan, Robert: poetic vocation, 127; inspiration, 127; work as self-expression, 129
DuRocher, Richard: *Milton and Ovid*, 9, 132

Education, 4, 5, 10; Milton's, 6, 17; limitations, 14, 20, 22, 125; curriculum, 18, 126, 138 (n. 8); debate, 47, 59; as common denominator, 125; methods, 126, 127
Eliot, T. S., 9, 58; purpose of poetic expression, 128; personal element in *The Waste Land*, 129
Elyot, Sir Thomas, 117
Epic, 108, 118
Erasmus, Desiderius: on education, 17; *Colloquies*, 24, 25, 35, 36, 64; "The Poetic Feast," 24, 25, 27; "De Rationii Studii," 100

Fink, Zera S., 48
Fowles, John: *Mantissa*, 129, 130, 131; Erato, 130; problems of creativity, 130
Fulgentius the Mythographer: Clio and learning, 106

Gafurius: *Practica Musica*, 114
Gardner, Dame Helen: Christianity of Milton's muse, 150 (n. 3); invocation of muse, 150 (n. 3)
Gathorne-Hardy, G. M.: "Destin'd Urn," 141 (n. 30)
Gauss, Karl Friedrich: on creativity, 71
Gilbert, Allan H.: dating *Samson Agonistes*, 146 (n. 12)
Gill, Alexander, the Younger, 22; Milton's correspondence with, 33, 70; influence on "To His Father," 140 (n. 16)

Index

Ginsberg, Allen: compliments Milton, 9, 129; "Blessed be the Muses," 129, 131; "Contest of Bards," 129, 131; use of muses, 130–31; poet as hero, 131; replacement of muses, 131; use of tradition, 132

Godwin, Thomas, 66, 67; *Roman Antiquities*, 65; use of pagan material, 65

Gossman, Ann: Siloam/Siloa's Brook, 149 (n. 17)

Grammar school, 4, 19, 21, 22, 24, 28, 40; exercises, 7, 34, 36, 128, 138 (n. 8); imitation, 10, 127, 136 (n. 22); curriculum, 31, 41, 139 (n. 13); reading, 35. *See also* St. Paul's School

Greek, 15, 17, 18, 19, 21, 22, 35, 51

Guillory, John: *Poetic Authority*, 9

Guisborough Statutes, 41

Gyraldus: *De Musis Syntagma*, 106

Hanford, James Holly, 9, 80

Hardison, O. B., Jr., 108

Harington, Sir John: translation of Ariosto, 122

Hazlitt, William, 2, 11; Milton's originality, 1

Hebrew, 18, 19

Hesiod, 28, 74, 108; *Theogony*, 2, 99, 100, 102, 104; muses, 2

Hobbes, Thomas, 11, 137 (n. 25); "Answer to the Preface to Gondibert," 12

Holdsworth, Richard, 36, 48; "Directions for a Student in the Universitie," 35, 41, 65; on university education, 35, 41

Homer, 1, 46, 58, 67; *Odyssey*, 59, 123; *Iliad*, 123

Hooker, Richard: *Laws of Ecclesiastical Polity*, 66, 67; Christian use of pagan tradition, 66

Hoole, Charles, 21; on educational limitations, 20; "The Master's Method," 25, 26, 41; language study, 26, 27, 29; poetic composition, 31, 51; curriculum, 41; *New Discovery of the Old Art of Teaching Schoole*, 101

Horace, 48, 57, 117

Hughes, Merritt Y., 103

Hunter, William B.: Urania synonymous with Jesus Christ, 94, 119

Hyginus: *Fabularum Liber*, 106

Inspiration, 2, 25, 49, 127; as madness, 64; divine, 82

Isaiah, 71

Isocrates, 39

Jaynes, Julian, 2

Jonson, Ben: "Over the Door at the Entrance into the Apollo," 49; muses, 49; on poetic inspiration, 49

Juvenal, 54, 57; third satire, 55; contrasts Roman republic and empire, 58

Kerrigan, William: *The Sacred Complex*, 9

Langdon, Ida: *Milton's Theory of Poetry and Fine Art*, 7

Language study, 1, 4, 16, 17, 18, 21, 22, 24, 26, 30; translation, 19, 26, 30; "turning," 19, 20, 138 (n. 8); composition, 19, 21, 36, 139 (n. 12); memorization, 20, 28, 36; grammar, 22, 25, 26, 28, 140 (n. 18). *See also* Greek; Hebrew; Latin

Latin, 1, 4, 17, 18, 19, 21, 22, 29, 30, 35, 36; Lily's grammar, 4, 19, 20, 22, 140 (n. 18); composition, 18, 29, 138 (n. 8)

Index

Lauter, Paul: Siloam/Siloa's Brook, 149 (n. 17)
Lily, William: Latin grammar, 4, 19, 20, 22, 140 (n. 18); "Carmen de Moribus," 19
Linocre, G.: *Musarum Libellum*, 99, 106
Linus, 58
Littleton, Dr. Adam: *Latine dictionary*, 108
Livius Andronicus: muses/camenae, 59
Livy, 54, 56
Low, Anthony, 60, 61
Lucretius, 28

MacKellar, Walter, 103; Milton's Latin poetry, 32; muse classification, 32, 33
Macrobius, 124; *Commentary on the Dream of Scipio*, 100
Maeonides, 74
Manso, Marquis of, 98, 109; "Manso" and, 52
Marino, 109
Marshall, William: frontispiece of *Poems*, 1645 edition, 112–14
Martial, 28
Martindale, Adam, 41; on educational limitations, 20; grammar school exercises, 128
Marvell, Andrew, 86
Masson, David, 60, 103
Mayerson, Philip: Orpheus and the muses, 154
Miller, James E., Jr., 129
Miller, Leo G.: Siloam/Siloa's Brook, 149 (n. 17)
Milton, Christopher (Milton's brother): on Milton's studiousness, 16
Milton, Elizabeth Minshull (Milton's third wife), 91
Milton, John, the Elder (Milton's father), 14, 16, 51, 107, 137 (n. 2); pretended dislike of poetry, 52; musicality, 137 (n. 3)
MILTON, JOHN: individuality, 1, 7, 10, 13, 37, 44, 72, 73, 74, 115, 132; inspiration, 4, 7, 45, 46, 51, 62, 71, 74, 79, 80, 83, 89, 92, 96, 120; *Paradise Lost*, 4, 5, 7, 12, 67, 69, 70, 73, 74, 79, 81, 83, 84, 85, 88, 89, 90, 91, 94, 95, 97, 112, 119, 120, 122, 124, 146 (n. 7), 148 (n. 17); Urania as his muse, 5, 12, 44, 70, 74, 95, 113, 120, 122, 123, 124, 125; education of, 6, 10, 14, 17, 21, 36, 46, 47, 50, 59, 96, 106, 126, 137 (n. 4); "Of Education," 7, 21; creativity, 7, 45, 71, 82; muses, 2, 4, 7, 32, 34, 42–53 passim, 59, 65, 67, 69, 89, 91, 94, 106, 107, 112, 119, 123; personality, 9, 14, 15, 16, 47, 60, 61, 74; juvenilia, 10; *Paradise Regain'd*, 13, 83, 95, 97; childhood, 14, 17; priestly vocation, 14, 75, 137 (n. 4); studiousness, 14, 15, 16, 22, 45, 47, 71, 75, 76, 80, 89, 138 (n. 9); correspondence, 15, 33, 70, 75, 80; reading, 15–16, 54, 64, 71, 82; language study, 16, 17, 22, 140 (n. 18); *Reason of Church Government*, 16, 31, 82, 89, 108; poetic composition, 16, 28, 31, 43, 45, 46, 63, 70, 71, 73, 76, 77, 80, 89, 90, 91, 92, 123, 124, 146 (n. 7); on education, 17, 21; on limitations of his education, 21, 22; grammar school, 22; "Elegy 4," 29, 97, 99, 105–06; "Elegy 6," 32, 37, 44, 45, 46, 48, 50, 51, 53, 58, 59, 61, 62, 70, 107, 143–44 (n. 21); "Lycidas," 32, 34, 60, 61, 101, 109, 121, 141 (n. 30); first prolusion, 34, 37, 38, 40, 42, 43; Cicero's *musae mansuetiores*, 37, 39, 42; use of

171

Index

mythology, 38, 67, 96; "L'Allegro," 38; "Il Penseroso," 38, 47, 107; contemporary audience, 40, 42; craftsmanship, 40; Nativity Ode, 44, 45, 46, 64, 67, 70, 79, 80, 92, 107, 119; *Poems*, 1645 edition, 44, 113; "To His Father," 51, 98, 99, 103, 106, 107, 140 (n. 16); "To Salsilli," 51, 52; "Manso," 51, 52, 98, 108; "Epitaph for Damon," 51, 53, 81, 84, 108; Italian journey, 52, 75; modesty, 52, 53, 57; autobiography in poetry, 60, 62, 63, 72, 143–44 (n. 21); use of tradition, 61, 73, 97, 132, 133; Christianity in poetry, 61, 67, 72, 75, 108, 112, 123; Psalm 114 translation, 70; blindness, 74, 86, 87, 88, 148 (n. 14); organization, 75, 76, 77, 79, 80; poetic vocation, 76, 148 (n. 14); Commonplace Book, 77; "At a Solemn Musick," 77; *First Defence of the English People*, 77, 84, 85; antiprelatical tracts, 77; divorce tracts, 77; marriages, 78–79, 84, 85, 91; poetic "drought," 79, 83–84; "Upon the Circumcision," 80; "The Passion," 80, 92; Arthuriad, 81, 112; Cadmon, 82; political activity, 82, 84; *Samson Agonistes*, 83, 146–47 (n. 12); "Ad Ioannem Rousium," 84; *Second Defence of the English People*, 84, 87; "On the New Forcers," 84; regicide, 86; Psalm 136, 92; Sonnet 7, 92; "Arcades," 101; *History of Britain*, 102; seventh prolusion, 103; Hammersmith period, 103; "At a Vacation Exercise," 107; "Elegy 1," 109; glory, 118; *Christian Doctrine*, 119–20; *Art of Logic*, 120; Blake's master, 127; kinship with Spenser, 128; celibacy vow, 147–48 (n. 14)

Milton, Katherine Woodcock (Milton's second wife), 85

Milton, Mary Powell (Milton's first wife), 84; desertion of Milton, 78–79

Milton, Sarah (Milton's mother), 14, 61, 137 (n. 2)

Minshull, Elizabeth. *See* Milton, Elizabeth Minshull

Mollenkott, Virginia: androgyny of Urania, 94

Moses: as poet, 121

MUSES, 2, 3, 4, 7, 13, 22, 32, 41, 47, 49, 51, 109, 152, 154; inspiration by, 2, 25, 27, 42, 63; Plato and, 3; Cicero and, 3, 42; rejection of, 3, 11, 135, 144; Urania, 5, 12, 44, 63, 67, 68, 69, 74, 91, 94, 95, 97, 112, 113, 114, 115, 116, 118, 119, 120, 121, 122, 123, 125; Clio, 10, 32, 75, 97, 98, 99, 102, 103, 104, 105, 106, 108, 109, 110, 111, 112, 113, 114, 115, 116, 118, 121, 122, 123, 152 (nn. 31, 41); Christian attitudes and uses, 11, 12, 63, 65, 66, 67, 69, 121, 144 (n. 29), 150 (n. 3); invocation, 12, 44, 83, 119, 150 (n. 3); connotations, 23, 28, 32, 33, 40, 42, 44, 50, 51; declensions, 23, 24, 32; definitions, 24, 28, 33, 42, 97; Calliope, 27, 28, 32, 75, 97, 99, 100, 101, 104, 105, 108, 122; epithets and synonyms, 27, 31, 32, 50, 51, 83, 94; classification, 32, 33, 34; Erato, 32, 46, 112, 130; Thalia, 32, 46; Melpomene, 32, 112; Terpsichore, 32; Euterpe, 27, 32; Polymnia, 32, 100; Polyhymnia, 32; functions, 34, 97, 99, 102, 103, 105, 108, 121,

172

Index

137 (n. 25); allusion to, 36, 43, 103, 106; "Heavenly Muse," 44, 45, 63, 65, 94, 95; Ben Jonson and, 49; wine associations, 49; Anacreon, 49; interchangeable with camenae, 59; "poetic madness," 64; creativity and, 71; Dame Memory and her siren daughters, 83; Orphean associations, 101; modern uses, 129, 130–31; replacement, 131

Numa, 54, 55

Oras, Ants: dating *Samson Agonistes*, 147
Origen, 5
Orpheus, 58, 101, 122, 152
Ovid, 11, 28, 29, 108, 132; Sandys's translation of *Metamorphoses*, 27, 100, 101; *Tristia*, 30; Tarpeian muse, 32; *Metamorphoses*, 48

Paideia group, 126
Parker, William Riley, 9, 40, 59, 73, 79, 103; *Milton*, 8; dating *Samson Agonistes*, 147 (n. 12)
Paulinus of Nola, 75; rejection of muses, 3
Phillips, Edward (Milton's nephew), 81, 92; on Milton, 14, 84, 90–91; on Mary Powell's desertion, 78–79
Plato, 31, 69, 82, 144 (n. 24); muses, 3; "Ion," 64; "Phaedrus," 64; *The Republic*, 100
Plutarch, 59; *De Pythiae Oraculis*, 102; role of muses, 121
Poetic composition, 6, 16, 19, 28, 30, 48, 138 (n. 8); Latin, 18, 29, 138 (n. 8); debate techniques and, 46; autobiography, 61, 62, 74; discipline, 63, 76, 80, 89, 92; revision, 90, 92; dictation,

90, 91; imitation, 127
Pound, Ezra, 9
Powell, Mary. *See* Milton, Mary Powell
Prose composition, 19, 29
Prudentius, 4, 67
Puritans, 11

Quilligan, Maureen: *Milton's Spenser*, 9
Quintilian: on literary borrowing, 37

Radzinowicz, Mary Ann: *Toward "Samson Agonistes,"* 9; dating *Samson Agonistes*, 147 (n. 12)
Raimondi, Marcantonio, 114, 116
Ralegh, Sir Walter, 66
Renwick, W. L., 100
Richardson, Jonathan, 61, 91; on Milton's poetic composition, 70
Rider's Latine Dictionary, 27
Ripa, Cesare: *Iconologia*, 105; Clio and glory, 105
Robbe-Grillet, Alain, 130
Robins, Harry F., 5
Robinson, Edwin Arlington: elegiac use of muses, 130
Ross, Alexander: *Mystagogus Poeticus*, 48, 65

Sadleir, Mrs. Anne: letter to Roger Williams, 86; regicide, 86; blindness as divine punishment, 86
St. Paul's School, 18, 23, 24, 35, 36; curriculum, 41, 138 (n. 8), 139 (n. 13), 141 (n. 21); school library books, 41, 104, 140 (n. 20). *See also* Grammar school
Salmasius, 6
Samuel, Irene, 64
Sandys, George: translation of Ovid's *Metamorphoses*, 27, 100, 101; Clio and glory, 105
Santayana, George: curricular

173

uniformity, 126
Sardanapalus, 47–48
Saurraute, Nathalie, 130
Scaliger, Julius Caesar, 48, 109; *Poetics*, 108; epic poetry, 108
Sedulius, 75
Sententiae Pueriles, 19
Shakespeare, William, 20, 38
Shawcross, John, 106; Clio's function, 102; dating *Samson Agonistes*, 147 (n. 12)
Siloam/Siloa's Brook, 149
Simonides, 102, 121, 124
Sirluck, Ernest: Milton and celibacy, 147–48 (n. 14)
Snare, Gerald: Siloam/Siloa's Brook, 149 (n. 17)
Socrates, 64
Spenser, Edmund, 4, 48, 67, 72, 107, 109, 124; *Teares of the Muses*, 69, 114; Christian muse, 69; "Virgilian progression," 77; *The Faerie Queene*, 77, 108, 117; *The Shepheardes Calendar*, 77, 99, 100; Milton and, 128; Clio as his muse, 108, 152 (n. 41)
Steadman, John M.: Milton's condemnation of epic tradition, 118
Stephanus, Carolus, 57, 58; *Dictionarium Historicum ac Poeticum*, 28, 56, 104; muses/camenae, 59
Stephanus, Robertus, 57, 58; *Thesaurus Linguae Latinae*, 4, 28, 41, 104; muses, 42, 58, 104
Stevens, Paul: *Imagination and the Presence of Shakespeare in Paradise Lost*, 9
Sylvester, Josuah, 68, 145 (n. 32); translation of Du Bartas, 67, 69

Tasso, 4, 61, 108, 109, 117
Terence, 26, 36
Thamyris, 74
Tillyard, E. M. W.: "L'Allegro" and first prolusion, 38; "Il Penseroso" and first prolusion, 38
Tireseas, 58, 85
Toland, John, 61
Tovey, Nathaniel, 36
Tradition, 1, 4, 10, 61, 73, 75, 97, 125, 132, 133; classical, 44, 117, 121; Christian, 44, 117, 121; blindness in, 74; transmission, 132
Trinity MS, 34, 77, 89, 90, 92, 101, 108, 122, 146 (n. 7)
Tully. *See* Cicero
Tuve, Rosemond, 2; Milton's originality, 1

University: exercises, 37. *See also* Cambridge
Urania. See Milton, John; Muses

Varro, 27, 58; on the Latin language, 56
Vida: *Christiad*, 80
Villey, Pierre: on blindness enhancing reflection, 89
Virgil, 11, 28, 29, 57, 67, 99, 100, 107, 117, 118; as "Virgin Poet," 48; "Virgilian progression," 76, 79; *Aeneid*, 122, 123
Vitruvius, 54; *On Architecture*, 55

Webber, Joan, 9
Whiting, George W.: Siloam/Siloa's Brook, 149
Williams, Roger, 86
Wittreich, Joseph Anthony, Jr.: *Visionary Poetics*, 9
Woodcock, Katherine. See Milton, Katherine Woodcock
Woodhouse, A. S. P., 103

Young, Thomas, 22, 28–29, 106, 107, 136 (n. 23); Milton's tribute to, 10, 97–98; Milton's "Elegy 4," 29; Milton's gratitude, 29

Zollikofer, Johannes, 87

About the Author

E. R. Gregory is Professor of English, University of Toledo.